A Matter of Spirit

Recovery of the Sacred in Contemporary Canadian Poetry

A Matter of Spirit

Recovery of the Sacred in Contemporary Canadian Poetry

Edited by Susan McCaslin

Ekstasis Editions

Canadian Cataloguing in Publication Data

Main entry under title:

A Matter of Spirit

ISBN 1-896860-24-9

1. Religious poetry, Canadian (English)* 2. Canadian poetry (English)--20th century.* I. McCaslin, Susan
PS8287.R4M37 1998 C811'.5408'0382 C98-911042-7
PR9195.85.R4M37 1998

Cover art: Hildegard von Bingen

Acknowledgments:
I wish to thank Douglas College for providing me with a year's educational leave in which to complete this anthology, and my publisher, Richard Olafson, for believing in it from the beginning. It also could not have been attempted without the support of my husband Mark, and my daughter, Claire, who were willing to share me with the computer for over a year. Appreciation to Mark Haddock, Mary Haddock, David Zieroth, Hannah Main-van der Kamp, Janet Allwork, and Celeste Schroeder for their astute editorial advice. Finally, I wish to thank the contributors for their enthusiasm regarding the value of such a project at this time.

Published in 1998 by:
Ekstasis Editions Canada Ltd.
Box 8474, Main Postal Outlet
Victoria, B.C. V8W 3S1

Ekstasis Editions
Box 571
Banff, Alberta T0L 0C0

The Canada Council for the Arts since 1957 | Le Conseil des Arts du Canada depuis 1957

A Matter of Spirit: Recovery of the Sacred in Contemporary Canadian Poetry has been published with the assistance of a grant from the Canada Council and the Cultural Services Branch of British Columbia.

Contents

A Matter of Spirit: *Recovery of the Sacred in Contemporary Canadian Poetry*

Interpreters and spoilers since the four
rivers flowed out of Eden,
men have nonetheless
learned that the Pure can bless
on earth and from on high
ineradicably.

Margaret Avison from "Light (III)"

We should conceive the identity of the various traditions, not by reconciling them through what they have in common, but by grasping the essence of what is specific in each. For the essence is one and the same.

Simone Weil from *Gateway to God*

In actual fact, every degree of materiality has its own function; and materiality extends in successive refinement until it becomes what has been generally considered to be separate—spirit.

Idries Shah from *The Sufis*

The Presence was spectrum-blue,
ultimate blue ray,

rare as radium, as healing;
my old self, wrapped round me,

was shroud (I speak of myself individually
but I was surrounded by companions

in this mystery)...

H.D. from "The Walls Do Not Fall" in *Trilogy*

Prayer is the Study of Art. Praise is the Practise of Art.

William Blake

He who tastes not, knows not.

Rumi

The words I speak to you, they are Spirit and they are life.

Jesus of Nazareth

The valley spirit never dies.
It is called the Mysterious Female.
And the doorway of the Mysterious Female
Is the base from which Heaven and Earth spring.
It is there within us all the time.
Draw upon it as you will, it never runs dry.

Lao Tzu from *Tao Te Ching*

INTRODUCTION:
A MATTER OF SPIRIT

Poetry is an entering into mystery, the zone of the unspeakable that desires to be spoken. At its deeper ranges, it is intimate with the mystical and with contemplative intuition. As a poet, scholar and instructor of English and Creative Writing, I have been intrigued for many years with the way language figures in the process of imaging or translating authentic spiritual experience. Since early childhood, my sense of the spiritual has been tied to inward experiences of a mystical nature, accompanied by intense bursts of creative energy. I have always assumed an intimate connection between human creativity and the creativity of a larger mind or "Creator Spirit." My own early Christian faith has been transformed radically, but the heart of it remains: a longing for union with a vast and mysterious realm that gives meaning and purpose to ordinary existence. From later immersion in British and European literary and mystical traditions, as well as a study of eastern and mid-eastern religions, I moved to the gradual discovery of an underground stream or subcurrent of Canadian poetry addressing such experience. Wilfred Campbell, Charles G.D. Roberts, Bliss Carman, Archibald Lampman, Duncan Campbell Scott, Marjorie Pickthall, A.M. Klein, Margaret Avison, Gwendolyn MacEwen and Bronwen Wallace are only a few of the poets who have contributed to this stream. This anthology originated out of a question about the relation between spirituality and poetry, and became in the end an exploration of the spiritual element in Canadian poetry.

Restrictions of time and space allow me to represent only a handful of contemporary Canadian poets, so I have focused on voices from a variety of cultural and religious backgrounds both within and without traditional religions. Some of these poets are working consciously within a particular sacred tradition, or are revisionist or syncretistic, while others are experimenting with new idioms and expressions outside recognized forms. Some writers are justifiably reluctant to give this element in their work a label or definition. After all, in Lao Tzu's words, "The way that can be spoken of/ Is not the true way."

Perhaps it is no coincidence that some of the poets represented find themselves standing outside or in resistance to orthodox systems of belief, yet indebted to the rich cultural and religious heritages in which they were born or to which they have later been exposed. The American psychologist Thomas Moore, in *The Re-Enchantment of Everyday Life*, defines spirituality as a sense of the sacred in the particulars of ordinary life, distinguishing it from most people's idea of religiosity: "I want to distinguish it [*Theos* in the older sense] from religion as an intellectual commitment buttressed by strong emotion and sheltered in an institution like a church or tradition." (Introd. xiv) He goes on to speak of the contemporary need to see the divine, "not as something set apart, but...the very heart and substance of everyday life."(313) Along with James Hillman, Robert Sardello and others writing today, he laments a loss of "soul" in our culture.

The contemporary poetic temperament, though soul-sick for the recovery of a sacred dimension within ordinary experience, is uncomfortable with dogma, didacticism, sentimentality, false piety, or abstraction—all of which have been associated with corrupt forms of institutional religion and with inferior "religious verse." Some of these poems express deep political and moral concerns about the uses to which religious ideology has been put, and question the historic role of religious institutions. This is not to say that great poetry cannot be written from within an orthodox religious tradition (consider Dante, Herbert, Hopkins, Thomas Merton), but that poets who do so, often challenge and expand the limits of officialdom.

The Vancouver journalist and religion editor, Douglas Todd, has cited recent polls that suggest at least ninety percent of North Americans say they believe in God or some kind of spiritual principle, while only about a third of the population regularly attends religious institutions. (1) The percentage of churchgoers is even lower in Canada. Out of this percentage of people committed to institutional religion, it is likely that artists and writers comprise an even smaller number, because of the way in which the creative mind resists and shatters "old wine skins."

In setting the works of poets from various spiritual traditions and outlooks side by side, I am not assuming that at root, all religions and spiritual paths are equivalent, but hoping the anthology will allow poems from various perspectives to converse. This anthology is not offered as a historical survey of religious verse or spiritual poetry in Canada, nor does it claim to be regionally representative. It is a beginning, an exploration, an opportunity for a handful of diverse Canadian poets to let their poetry, accompanying interviews and short prose pieces speak for themselves about this matter of "spirit." Like the poems of the great religious traditions of east and west, the poems here resound in voices of prayer, confession, meditation, contemplation, lament, praise, adoration, lyric exuberance, aphorism, and ecstatic utterance. As contemplative writer Kathleen Norris has said, "Poetry, like prayer, is a dialogue with the sacred." (64)

Poems of longing for spirit often hinge on paradox, suggestion, word play, obliquity, and it is so here. These poems demonstrate a love of language, words and naming, yet a sense of the limitations of language; a feeling for what can and cannot be spoken about the divine. Many embody the paradox that we cannot know the mystery at the heart of things with the discursive mind or rational intellect, but that we can experience it directly, if only for fleeting instants. Some hint that the ground of our individual being and that of the cosmos connect or are one.

The poetic images in this collection embrace the quotidian, the everyday particulars of time and place, the murkiness and irresolution of life lived in time. They explore the unpredictable journeying of the "soul," an unfashionable word I'd like to reclaim as the localized, embodied form of spirit, that which mediates between the realms of spirit and matter. Many of the poems imply that the unavoidable and appropriate path to integration lies in descending into experience, rather than in escaping prematurely to a transcendence outside or beyond the world. Yet there is also an insistence that things are both themselves and grounded in a reality beyond themselves. The old quarrel between those who claim the divine is transcendent and those who focus on the immanent is partly addressed here by poems that insist on both. The divine is within, without, encompassing, here, now, beyond. It is in the "divine particulars of grace," as Bronwen Wallace called them, that Being makes its presence felt for embodied beings. Certainly in entering the worlds of these poems one engages profound questions of epistemology, ontology, teleology—what can we know? how can we *be* in the world? is there a purpose to existence? This is poetry that listens, moving beyond the materialism and commercialism of our culture.

In assembling these selections, I was particularly engaged by poems that seemed at root, ontological—work that moves through longing toward some kind of union of the personal, individual self with an interconnected whole—whether identified as God, the Goddess, Creator, Being, the Self, Presence, the Beloved, Mystery, Numinosity, Nature, or a cosmological power that must remain nameless, unnameable. The vocabulary for this energetic, erotic, dynamic creative source or centre of both world and self varies, as does the willingness or unwillingness to name it. I was after poetic configurations of those moments of epiphany or presence that suggest something irreducible behind or within the play of appearances. I was engaged by poems that expressed spiritual struggle, *agon*, even resistance to tradition and religious heritage, longing, homesickness—a desire to reclaim a space where mind and world, body and soul, self and God (or the Goddess, the gods) were distinguishable, but not posed as irreconcilable opposites. I was moved by poems that seemed to proceed out of some kind of profound personal experience of a sacred energy in the world, nature, the self, and in words or language larger than the individual ego—the Other voice that mystics say is closer than one's jugular vein, "nearer than hands and feet, closer than breathing." Like Julian of Norwich, many of these poets link this sense of Spirit to a presence of divine Love that whispers in the inner ear, "All shall be well," a phrase echoed at the end of Dennis Lee's confessional meditation, "Nightwatch."

So far, the language I have been using to describe the poetic embodiment of spiritual yearning (not necessarily spiritual arrival) is abstract, philosophical, metaphysical, not the language of poetry. Poetry may incorporate the abstract, the intellectual, but expresses itself in metaphor, image, verbal play, resonance, musicality. Like Emily Dickinson, it tells the truth, but "tells it slant." The poems here imply, more than state; suggest, more than preach; whisper and chant and sing, more than teach.

Often, discussion of spiritual matters gets bogged down in questions of belief, that which can be affirmed or denied (credal formulations, religious dogma, "I'm right, you're wrong" thinking). Poetry, on the other hand, has always been able to deal in paradox, to hold polarities in an active balance. Poets tend to rely rather on what can be intuited, experienced and integrated into daily life. Some forms of postmodern theory have inhibited the conversation about soul and its relation to spirit by arguing that notions of the soul, spirit, the integral self, are merely cultural and social constructs and therefore ultimately meaningless. The poems in this volume bring the experiential dimension of the sacred back into the conversation as a reality of perception. It is encouraging that we are beginning to see "reconstructive" postmodernist theory emerging at this time. In *Sacred Interconnections: Postmodern Spirituality, Political Economy, and Art,* for instance, editor David Ray Griffin writes:

> The postmodernism of this series can be called constructive or revisionary. It seeks to overcome the modern world view not by eliminating the possibility of world views as such, but by constructing a postmodern world view through a revision of modern premises and traditional concepts. This constructive or revisionary postmodernism involves a new unity of scientific, ethical, aesthetic, and religious intuitions. (Introd. x)

The more skeptical deconstructionists are correct that we are in large part constructs of our culture, language and environment. And certainly there is value in the "ground-clearing" questioning of closed ideologies. Yet the old vocabulary of the soul's hidden mysteries may still have something to reveal. Poetry tells us we are much more, not less, than such constucts. Perhaps the extreme materialism and consumerism of Western culture is having the reverse effect of turning us back upon our inner resources, those regions from which poetry arises.

The dominant skeptical mode of twentieth century poetry and poetics has translated into a dominantly ironic poetic voice. Yet the poems in this volume have opened themselves once more to joy, hope, solemnity, ecstasy, lamentation and praise, that is, the full range of the human "feeling intellect" (Coleridge's term). In such a context, faith and doubt are not mutually exclusive. Many of these poems are politically and socially critical, without relinquishing celebration and a love of the natural and supernatural worlds.

The thrust of much deconstruction theory has been to question radically the notion of exhaustive metaphysical systems. Yet in one sense this is what poetry has always done—taken us out into the open, pushed us up against the limits of language. While deconstruction can end in nihilism, it can also return us to a dialogue with meaning and presence. Buddhism also leads to a radical questioning of ideology and language; yet the emptiness of the monk and the mystic, the emptiness at the heart of most traditional mystic paths, is an opening to compassion, joy and equanimity, not a closure into an abyss of meaninglessness or despair.

Many of the poets in this volume turn to nature for inspiration and a renewal of faith. The old notion of nature standing below, and God above the human and natural realms (the hierarchical Chain of Being), has given way in recent ecological and feminist thinking to the non-Cartesian view that humans need to place themselves back within the order of nature. Neither is nature to be viewed merely as an occasion for our reflexive thinking. Writers like theologian Matthew Fox have articulated an earth-centered or "creation spirituality," tied to what Fox calls "panentheism"—the sense that God (or the Spirit) and nature interpenetrate, rather than collapsing into each other, as in simple pantheism. Whatever the views of particular poets on such issues, a humbler and more reverential attitude toward the natural world as sacred space emerges in many of these poems. Robert Bringhurst's short prose piece, for example, makes an argument for wilderness based on spiritual presence.

A year spent with these poems has enabled me to identify the following emergent themes or directions in "inspirited" Canadian poetry: 1) a sense of the interconnectedness and interdependency of all things, 2) an opening to feminine metaphors for the divine and revisionist approaches to biblical stories, 3) a valuation of nature leading into a radically non-dualistic nature poetry (less anthropocentric) which transcends Romanticism or perhaps transforms its legacy, and 4) a sense that mystical or contemplative awareness and socio-political concern are not dualities, but poles of a single awareness.

It remains to say a few specific words about the contributors. The diversity of the poets is evident, but on typing their poems into my computer, I was struck by the parallels, resonances and echoes among them. It was as if the poems were speaking a common language in various dialects.

The poems of Dennis Lee and Tim Lilburn unite what the Medievals called the "via negativa" (or apophatic tradition) and the "via positiva." The "via negativa" questions the ability of words and images to translate the divine into human terms. Each naming is simultaneously an unnaming or negation. Yet the "via positiva" insists that metaphor can "bring across" the divine. Their poems suggest that the phrase, "This is thou; this is not thou," must be uttered in a single breath. Spiritual growth comes out of humility, unknowing, silence, emptying (kenosis), a "dark night of the soul," a refusal or loss of language, so that words may return and flourish in more authentic contexts. As Thomas Merton puts it,

> ...in all these higher religious traditions the path to transcendent realization is a path of ascetic self-emptying and "self-naughting" and not at all a path of self-affirmation, of self-fulfilment, or of perfect attainment." (76)

As one who trained for the Jesuit priesthood, Lilburn is explicit about his interaction with his predecessors in a long and vital tradition (the desert Fathers, pseudo-Dionysius, the anonymous author of *The Cloud of Unknowing,* Eckhart etc.); whereas Lee, though equally aware of mystical and religious tradition, speaks as a secular man struggling in the dark to purify his life, waiting on absence to become presence without giving it a name. In some of the longer meditative poems represented here, Lee interweaves confession, meditation and contemplation. Lilburn's rush of images, and tumbling, ecstatic celebration of the sensuous, physical world in his early poems, yields in *Moosewood Sandhills* to a much quieter and more contemplative voice, in which images of deer, grass, hills, desert recur with gentle, rhythmic insistence. In one of the last poems in the series, the speaker expresses his desire to lie within the spine of a deer—dwelling alongside its strangeness and otherness.

Robin Skelton's work takes us into the world of Wicca, associated with pre-Christian matriarchal rites and the religious practices of the ancient Celts. He revives feminine images for the divine, the Goddess or Muse, the use of magic, incantation and spell—the poetry of music and enchantment. This content, combined with a formidable mastery of poetic forms, allows him to tap the deeper rhythms of the spirit. I was most privileged to be able to interview Robin shortly before his death in August of 1997. Apparently, this interview was one of his last literary acts "on the record" before he died.

Miriam Waddington and Leonard Cohen, in very different ways, have remained true to their Jewish cultural and religious backgrounds. Cohen's poems, especially in the selections from *The Book of Mercy*, are modern psalms offering a broken self to the Hebrew God of Mercy. These poems, both traditional and innovative in form and content, were perhaps neglected on their first publication due to the unfashionableness of religious poetry. Yet they and the more popular songs (which are not separable from the poetry), move out of silence, meditation, and a unique amalgamation of Zen Buddhist practice and Jewish metaphor.

Waddington's early exposure to Yiddish tales and stories, and her background as a social worker in Montreal, coalesce in poems of acute perception of everyday life that are often social criticisms. The lyrical voice and the voice of social concern are unified in her work. Though she would not call herself a "visionary" or a "prophet," she joins with the Hebrew prophet Amos in "A Morning Like the Morning When Amos Awoke" to call for the "raining down" of justice. There is a deep sense of exile and human fragmentation in her work, mitigated by a strong belief in poetry as a larger force moving through the individual who is called to it as a vocation—the poet as vessel.

Elizabeth Brewster, like Waddington, is fascinated by Old Testament figures and biblical stories. Her poems on Dinah and Tamar take little-known biblical women and retell their stories in ways that offer insight into the survival and strength of feminine consciousness within a patriarchal culture. Her recent sequence, "Footnotes to the Book of Job," reenacts the timeless problem of evil and suffering within a contemporary context, and offers the reader a fresh image of God as "not a theologian/ but a wild poet."

Ajmer Rode's aphoristic lyrics, as well as his longer metaphysical meditations, draw from the great Hindu sacred texts such as the Vedas, Upanishads, and the Bhagavad-Gita. Some of his poems are translated from his original Punjabi, but much of his work is composed in English. He is also fascinated, like Teilhard de Chardin, with the correlation between science and poetry, assuming that greater penetration of the secrets of matter may enhance our sense of the mystery and sacredness of life. Like some quantum physicists curious about the metaphysical implications of matter at the sub-atomic level, he is alert to the strangeness and unpredictability of matter, and speculates on such questions as how to draw a line between what is animate and inanimate.

With Blake, his poetry declares that "everything that lives is holy." In his short essay he articulates the need for compassion, the sense that a spirituality devoid of a sense of care for the world rings hollow.

Lorna Crozier and Barry Dempster are grappling in very different ways with their Christian religious heritages, partly through rejection and radical transformation. Some of Crozier's recent work takes well-known biblical stories, like that of the seven-day creation, or Noah and his unnamed wife, and retells them from a feminist perspective. She is something of a polytheist or pagan (in the sense of "country dweller") in her perception of nature and refusal to separate the divine from the world of prairie or Vancouver Island landscape. Her poems force us to examine the inner world of dreams and myth; to look at angels as mysterious powers operative within nature and the human being. Her work demonstrates a continual effort to reclaim the feminine body and voice and connect them to the voice and body of the world.

Barry Dempster's recent poems from *Fire and Brimstone* take us into the strange and fantastical world of his fundamentalist upbringing in the Plymouth Brethren Church, and through his later discovery of poetic mentors and predecessors for whom metaphor and symbol were not profanations. He recovers Jesus the poet, and begins a spiritual quest that leads him to fuse himself with D.H. Lawrence as persona, and enter Lawrence's exotic New Mexican experience before his death where the old gods of the Mayans speak for the sensual soul. Dempster is critical of his own religious upbringing, but recognizes it as the source of many of his images. In much poetry of resistance, there is a double movement of love/hate, a sense that the poet must be free, yet honour the community or experience from which he or she has emerged.

The two First Nations' poets in the collection take varying approaches to their rich native heritages. Sky Dancer Louise B. Halfe has written eloquently in prose about the travesty of the Canadian residential school system that stripped her people of their language and dignity, and some of her poems address the historic injustices of the Church and the impact of Christianity on her community. She has responded by returning to her native Cree rituals, language and traditions. Her work is deeply integrated because of her spiritual focus which honours the elders, the dances, the songs, the ceremonies, and reconnects her with the world of ancestral and animal spirits, the grandmothers and grandfathers with whom her poetry communes.

Poet and playwright Daniel David Moses, who was brought up within an Anglican church mission on his reserve, suspects that his attitudes are a mixof Christianity and traditional Iroquoian cultural norms. Though he sees himself as less consciously focused than Halfe on his native spiritual heritage, his work too explores the feminine through his obsession with the moon, and the delicate connection between body and spirit. There is also a recurring theme of the persistence and tenacity of native ways in poems like "The Persistence of Songs" and "Grandmother of the Glacier."

P.K. Page has long been recognized as a modern metaphysical poet, but critics are just beginning to recognize the Sufic underpinnings of some of her work, as in the poem "At Sea" where the Sufi poet Rabia appears. However, she also draws from a wide variety of traditions from both east and west. According to Idries Shah, Sufism is not a belief system, but a way of being, a mystical path that has to be experienced and cannot be preached. He distinguishes the Sufic way from conventional religion:

> First of all, you must realize that what ordinary man calls "spirituality" is usually a vague aspiration towards something "higher," or perhaps an indulgence in certain forms of emotion, hallowed only by custom, because of their historical or associative connection with what have been assumed or claimed for a long time to be spiritual things. We are not working with this false element at all. (239)

For Page, the esoteric aspect of many of the great religions meet to form a powerful underground stream, what Aldous Huxley called the "Perennial Philosophy," but she eschews labels and even terms like "spirituality," preferring the term "cosmological" to describe what she is after. Certainly, many of her poems are haunted by metaphors of optics and seeing, and given that she is also a splendid visual artist, the use of the seeing eye that reaches behind images to what she calls "unrefractive whiteness," is highly appropriate. In "Chinese Boxes" she speaks of "that inner eye/ which sees the absolute/ in emptiness." Many of her poems enact a quest for a spiritual dimension hidden within or behind appearances. In others, observer and observed, knower and known, cannot be separated (see "Three Gold Fish"), and in some she writes of how art enfolds us within a larger pattern or design. "Planet Earth," one of the most moving of the poems in her recent book, *Hologram: A Book of Glosas,* is a rich gloss on lines by Neruda that takes up the notion of our guardianship of the earth through domestic metaphors of laundering, ironing—a loving paean.

The work of Robert Bringhurst draws together many pre-Christian philosophical and wisdom traditions—those of the Pre-Socratics, ancient Chinese poets and sages, Buddhism (including Zen), as well as the North American native languages and literatures through his study of the Haida. The selections from his recent collection, *The Calling,* include chiselled lyrics as well as longer narrative poems that draw us into a world where paradox and surprise fling us into new modes of perceiving. He is able to fuse his voice with those of his ancient sources to create a reversal of our usual preconceptions about spirit, and with Lilburn and Lee, his obsessions are profoundly ontological. Truth is to be found not just in the sublime and exalted, but in the physical, the dark, the profane. He challenges our usual separation of the secular and the sacred:

> Stones and trees are my teachers, but
> there are others. The truth of the world
> sparkles in slopbuckets, toilet bowls, turds
> and in festering sores.
>
> Are your eyes plugged up with light
> your ears plugged up with music
> and your nose with sweet spring air?
> Everything that has ever existed is medicine.
> (from "Yunmen Wenyan")

Anne Szumigalski, Sharon Thesen, and David Zieroth are poets whose work also reclaims the world of the everyday for spirit and forces us to see the familiar as unfamiliar. Szumigalski's use of surrealism and powerfully imaged dream-like sequences takes us into a Blakean, non-dualistic Gnostic world that reverses conventional religious ideology. Some of her sources are Blake and the Gnostic Gospel of Thomas. The forbidden fruit, the resurrection, paradise are configured in new and startling ways. Like Crozier's work, hers is full of angels, and (like Crozier's) they are not the tame and cuddly cherubs of Baroque art:

> ...have you noticed
> how they roost in trees?
> not like birds
> their wings fold the other way... (from "Angels")

Sharon Thesen's crafted poems layer ancient myth (cosmology) with the mundane as in the poem "Aurora" where the ancient goddess of dawn is the feminine hiddenness behind appearances, the invisible in the visible:

> Garland remains of the starry dynamo surround her
>
> Galactic waterfall shreds & threads over stone
>
> And stone steep downward, the many kilowatts

Feed cites, farms, basement operations.

Yet in "Easter Sunday" and "The Stone" she revisits Christian myth:

Those silent rows of monks
come out from solitary
to labour over a complicated beauty—
how did they feel
patiently gilding the garments
& long hair of those two women
who with hands folded or clenched
in grief watch the solemn volunteers
push the stone
across the door
to his body.
(from "The Stone")

David Zieroth's probing narrative and confessional poems explore the contemporary, fragmented self within an urban landscape. Many of his poems revitalize the metaphor of the journey, whether the journey from prairie to west coast, the dream journey, the journey from youth to mid-life, or the daily journey to and from work. Yet his recent work moves toward states of perception that infer the individual's presence within a much larger, more comprehensive and gracious order:

...we smell the river
and are grateful although
its raw red line
can reek of sewage, more
risk in this long life on a small planet
judged to be scientifically alone
even as our hi-tech runners
scuff along the bank
and our inner chemistry
strains hugely for
some cosmological love
untouched by how we change.
(from "The Poplars of St. Vital")

His poem "Question" is one of the most explicit in this volume in addressing open-endedly the more profound questions about the soul, embodiment, immortality, life-after death, that secretly haunt us all but often go unspoken:

> My own soul,
> did it grow out of childhood or was it bestowed?

In the reverberation of such questions, it is time to observe the wisdom of the sages and enter silence, letting the poems speak finally for themselves.

Susan McCaslin
January 1997

WORKS CITED

Griffin, David Ray, ed. *Sacred Interconnections: Postmodern Spirituality, Political Economy, and Art.* Albany, N.Y.: State University of New York Press, 1990.

Merton, Thomas. *Zen and the Birds of Appetite.* N.Y.: New Directions, 1968.

Moore, Thomas. *The Re-Enchantment of Everyday Life.* N.Y.: Harper Collins, 1996.

Norris, Kathleen. *The Cloister Walk.* New York: Riverhead Books, 1996.

Shah, Idries. *The Commanding Self.* London: The Octagon Press, 1994.

Todd, Douglas. *Brave Souls: Writers and Artists Wrestle with God, Love, Death and the Things that Matter.* Toronto: Stoddart, 1996.

Elizabeth Brewster

ELIZABETH BREWSTER was born in Chipman, New Brunswick in 1922. She has lived in Alberta, British Columbia, and Ontario, as well as in the United States and England. Since 1972 she has lived in Saskatoon, Saskatchewan, where she taught at the University of Saskatchewan until 1990. She is now professor Emeritus. She has published twenty-two books, the most recent being *Away from Home* (prose), *Footnotes to the Book of Job* (poetry), and *Garden of Sculpture* (poetry). *Footnotes to the Book of Job* was shortlisted for the Governor General's Award for poetry for 1996. Also in 1996 she was presented with a Lifetime Award for Excellence in the Arts from the Saskatchewan Arts Board. Previous awards included the E.J. Pratt Award for poetry from the University of Toronto, 1953; the President's Medal and Award for Poetry (best magazine poem) from the University of Western Ontario, 1979; D. Litt., University of New Brunswick, 1982; *Spring Again* (1991) was shortlisted for the Pat Lowther Award for Poetry, League of Canadian poets.

For the unknown goddess

Lady, the unknown goddess,
we have prayed long enough only
to Yahweh the thunder god.

Now we should pray to you again
goddess of a thousand names and faces
Ceres Venus Demeter Isis
Inanna Queen of Heaven
or by whatever name
you would be known

you who sprang from the sea
who are present in the moisture of love
who live in the humming cells
of all life
who are rain
with its million soft fingers

and you who are earth
you with your beautiful ruined face
wrinkled by all
that your children have done to you

sunlike lady
crowned with the whirling planets.

Lady of peace, of good counsel,
of love, of wisdom

we invoke your name
which we no longer know

and pray to you
to restore our humanity
as we restore your divinity.

ELIZABETH BREWSTER

Creation

It is said that when God created the universe
he did not employ the angels
but the twenty-two letters of the Hebrew alphabet
and the ten numbers.

I imagine letters squiggling gaily
across the sky,
shaping themselves into words,
creating the sun and moon and stars.

The letters issued
out of the invisible mouth
of the unknowable God.
Bound together as words
they invented everything
shiny and new as the objects
in this child's Hebrew primer,
where I see, beside the letters,
cats, dogs, mice, lions, turtles,
a great dragon, a computer,
a man flying a kite,
ladders reaching up to a space-ship,

a surprised fisherman
hauling in the great Leviathan itself.

Dinah and Her Brethren

What did Dinah think?
That's the question
to which there seems to be no answer.

It's not even quite clear
exactly what happened.

Everybody knows about the sons of Jacob,
Joseph and his brethren
(the story of all that envy, treachery, forgiveness).

Dinah was the daughter,
the one her mother Leah prayed for
after all her sons had been born.

Of course she was beautiful,
as daughters in stories so often are.

Jacob once hid her in a chest
so that his brother Esau
would not see her and desire her.

And a day came when Dinah
went out to visit
the daughters of the land.

Just a social call?
An interest in the goddesses
of the Canaanite women?

The legend says there were parades
with dancing women,
a high festival.

And the eye of the young
Canaanite chieftain Shechem
fell upon Dinah.

Did he rape her,
carry her off by force,
or did she consent?

Whatever happened,
she was disgraced
in the eyes of her family.

To be just to Shechem,
he wanted to marry Dinah.
He spoke tenderly to the girl,
asked her father's permission
(rather late, it must be admitted),
offered a high bride-price.

And Jacob agreed, however grudgingly,
making the best (he may have thought)
of a bad job.
(Who else, after this,
would marry the girl?)

But the brothers came in from the fields
and they were angry.

Still, they too seemed to accept,
only demanding
that Shechem and his relatives and townsmen
should all be circumcised.
And Shechem agreed,
managed to persuade his kinsmen.

Three days after the circumcision,
Simeon and Levi, two of Dinah's brothers,
killed Shechem and all his kin.
Some of the other brothers
pillaged and burned the town.

Here the legends disagree.
One legend says
that Dinah had sent a message to her brothers,
summoned them to her aid.

Another legend says
that the brothers had to tear her
forcibly from Shechem
before they killed him
and carried her home with them.

So you can imagine her a Lucrece
urging her brothers to revenge
her cruel dishonour

or a Juliet crossed in love
for one outside her tribe.

Either way, an Elizabethan poet
would have opened her heart for us
and made her eloquent.

But Dinah says nothing.

Still, unlike Lucrece and Juliet,
she goes on living, is perhaps braver,
after all, than they are.

In the Torah, she goes down to Egypt
with her father and brothers,
and is never mentioned again.

In one of the legends, however,
she is married to Job.

Not the wife who said to Job,
"Curse God and die,"
but the mother of his second family,
seven sons and three beautiful daughters
(Jemimah, Keziah, Keren-happuch)
Job's consolations in old age.

Poetic justice, to link
these two survivors,
Job and Dinah,
give them an autumnal happy ending.

Did Dinah ever tell her daughters
(maybe after their uncles visited)
about her tragic youth?
Or did she keep her own counsel,
more patient than Job?

Maybe there is a tribe of Dinah,
as well as the tribes of Reuben, Levi, Judah,
Joseph and all those others:

a tribe of women, still
mysteries to their brothers.

Tamar's Story

Surely God prefers tricksters:

sly Rebecca and smooth Jacob
rather than the dutiful Isaac
or the sturdy hunter Esau;

also the Canaanite woman Tamar,
tricking her father-in-law Judah
(Jacob's son)
into her bed,
thus becoming
the ancestress of David
and David's royal, Messianic line.

No dimity heroine, Tamar:
a strong, devious woman
who knew what she wanted
and set out to get it.

How much she must have wanted children.
None by her first husband,
or by his brother, her second husband.
She is not given the third brother in marriage,
though he has been promised to her,
and what is she to do?

After all, that family owes her a child.

Her thoughts turn to Judah, her father-in-law,
lately a widower,
still a strong man
in spite of his years,
not like those weaklings,
her dead husbands.

She sits by the wayside,
dressed like a prostitute, her face veiled,
when Judah comes by.

What was she thinking, I wonder?
Was she frightened?
confident or desperate?
Did she need to put on a good act
or was Judah easily fooled,
half-drunk, perhaps,
or not seeing much in the evening dusk
after a long day's sheepshearing?

Not many words between them,
only that he promises
a kid from his flock,
and leaves with her,
as surety for his payment,

his seal and his ring and the stick he carries.

Later, he tries to send her the kid,
but the woman cannot be found.
Nobody knows who she is.

For Tamar, it's a dangerous triumph.

Pregnant, she is accused
of having acted the wanton
and could be burned to death.

But she provides Judah's ring and seal
as proof of her child's parentage.

A strange recognition scene
it must have been,
big-bellied Tamar
confronting Judah.

"She was in the right," he said,
"more righteous than I."

No love story, this,
though Judah may have felt
some wary respect for Tamar.
If they lived happily ever after,
it was not together.

But Judah's tribe did not die out,
and Tamar had her twin sons,
her heart's desire.

From these two, in later generations,
came royal David,
the shepherd king,
brave, lustful, devout, unscrupulous,
harpist, poet, singer of songs

God's beloved son
and true descendant of Tamar.

from *"Footnotes to the Book of Job"*

1

Late November, Advent at hand

treacherous streets
after a freezing rain.

I stay home Sunday morning,
drink coffee, turn the pages.

The book reads backward,
Hebrew on the right of the page,
English on the left.

The foreign alphabet incomprehensible
reminds me
how distant this time,
this place

the land of Uz
on the edge of desert
where Job lives with his flocks,
a man wealthy in camels
and sheep and oxen

his sons and daughters
feasting like young princes

a splendour,
simple and barbarous

God also, in a splendid
and barbarous heaven,
is visited one day
by all his sons,
and among them the Satan,
adversary, tester, observer

servant of God.

And there is a bet in heaven.
God bets on Job,
the Satan against him.

4

Job is plagued with boils
(elephantiasis, maybe? black leprosy?)
I conjure up all physical ailments:
cancer, perhaps, AIDS, perhaps.
His flesh and bones suffer,
his breath is foul,
he has bad dreams.
He seems near to death,
but cannot die.

"Curse God and die," his wife says,
but he does not
yet.

18

God is not a theologian
but a wild poet
delighting in cloud and thunder,
in eagle and raven,

variety, struggle, the leap
in the dark for prey
(or the delicate wing of the butterfly).

Is God to be tamed
to civilized
predictability?

Who has the right to demand
that God be just?

19

Was Incarnation God's
answer to Job?

Did God yearn
to share the life of his creatures?
Be shut in, confined
in flesh and bone?
Feel cold, heat, hunger,
the pang of ambition?
Job's boils?

But why be a man?
Why not a lion,
an eagle, a snake?

Was it human language
he wanted, baby talk
from his mother, after the cold
music of stars?

An Interview With Elizabeth Brewster (March 1997)

SM: What kind of religious upbringing, if any, did you experience, and how has it shaped you as a poet?

EB: My mother was brought up as a Baptist, though she joined the Anglican Church because my father was an Anglican. I was taken to both the Baptist and the Anglican churches, so I had that experience of hearing hymns and so on. Also, the Prayer Book I found quite beautiful. Because I spent several years of my childhood in the country and we didn't have very many books, the Bible was one of the books I had, and I remember reading the whole Bible by the time I was twelve. It is a beautiful group of books; and the favourite ones I came back to many times—the Psalms, Ecclesiastes and Job.

SM: You have written a number of poems about biblical women figures from the Old Testament. Could you talk a bit about those poems.

EB: Several of the poems you have chosen for the anthology are based either on the bible or on Jewish legends. I suppose I have come back to these biblical or near-biblical stories because they connect with my earlier influences. I learned to read from a book of Bible stories with an alphabet at the front; and I can still close my eyes and see some of the illustrations in that book: Adam and Eve in the Garden of Eden, Noah's Ark, Lot's wife turned to a pillar of salt, Joseph and his brethren, baby Moses in the bulrushes with the Egyptian princess bending over him, the Israelites in the desert with the Golden Calf. Also, my mother used to read a chapter of the Bible aloud in the evenings; and, as I was the youngest child, I used to sit on her knee and turn the pages for her.

The Book of Job is, of course, one of the most beautiful and controversial books of the Bible, dealing with that ever-recurring problem, "If God is good, why do bad things happen to good people?" The stories of Dinah and Tamar are interesting human stories, but not the sort you would likely run into in Sunday School. Dinah was mentioned briefly in a Jewish feminist book, Judith Plaskow's *Standing Again at Sinai;* and I looked her up in the bible and in books of Jewish legends, where I was intrigued to see her mentioned as Job's second wife. Tamar's story was called to my attention in Harold Bloom's essay in *The Book of J* (edited by David Rosenberg and Harold Bloom). Bloom speaks of her as his favourite heroine from those early stories. The legend behind

"Creation" pleased me. A lover of words is bound to enjoy the thought that "in the beginning were the letters." I think that I have always been a seeker, and many of my poems through the years have been connected with that source.

SM: Whether you are drawing from biblical or classical sources, your poems seem to explore spiritual issues and states. Do you see the creative impulse and the spiritual impulse as related in any way?

EB: I think the creative impulse often comes from letting yourself go, and I suppose prayer, like poetry, is a kind of opening up. Whether it is an inner voice or an outer voice, it's an opening out.

Robert Bringhurst

ROBERT BRINGHURST was born in the infamous hothouse of south central Los Angeles in 1946 and brought to Canada as an immigrant in 1952. He was raised primarily in Alberta, and since 1972 has lived on the coast of British Columbia. He has published more than a dozen books of poetry. The most comprehensive of these is *The Calling: Selected Poems 1970-1995* (McClelland & Stewart, 1995). Many of his recent poems are polyphonic compositions for two, three or four simultaneous voices. Trained as both a linguist and an art historian, he has studied Native American languages and oral literatures extensively. His major work in this field is *A Story as Sharp as a Knife: An Introduction to Classical Haida Literature* (1997). His writings on the history of art include *The Black Canoe* (2nd ed., 1992) and *Elements of Typographic Style* (2nd ed., 1996).

Poem About Crystal

Look at it, stare
into the crystal because
it will tell you, not
the future, no, but
the quality of crystal,
clarity's nature,
teach you the stricture
of uncut, utterly
uncluttered light.

Deuteronomy

The bush. Yes. It burned like they say it did.
Lit up like an oak in October—except
that there is no October in Egypt. Voices
came at me and told me to take off my shoes,
and I did that. That desert is full of men's shoes.
And the flame screamed, *I am what I am.*
I am whatever it is that is me,
and nothing can but something needs to be
done about it. If anyone asks,
all you can say is, What is is what sent me.

I went. But I brought my brother to do
the talking, and I did the tricks—the Nile
full of fishguts and frogs, the air opaque
and tight as a scab, the white-hot hail,
and boils, and bugs, and when nothing had worked right,
we killed them and ran. We robbed them of every
goddamned thing we could get at and carry
and took off, and got through the marsh at low tide
with the wind right, and into the desert. The animals
died, of course, but we kept moving.

Abraham came up easy. We took
the unknown road and ate hoarfrost and used
a volcano for a compass. I had no plan.
We went toward the mountains. I wanted, always,
to die in the mountains, not in that delta.
And not in a boat, at night, in swollen water.
We travelled over dead rock and drank dead water,
and the hoarfrost wasn't exactly hoarfrost.
They claimed it tasted like coriander,
but no two men are agreed on the taste
of coriander. Anyway,
we ate it. And from time to time we caught quail.

Men and half-men and women, we marched
and plodded into those hills, and they exploded
into labyrinths of slag. The air licked us
like a hot tongue, twisting and flapping and gurgling
through the smoke like men suffocating or drowning, saying,
An eye for an eye, and on certain occasions
two eyes for one eye. Either way, you model me
in thin air or unwritten words, not in wood,
not in metal. I am gone from the metal when the metal
hits the mould. You will not get me into any image
that will not move when I move, and move
with my fluency. Moses! Come up!

I went. But I wore my shoes and took a waterskin.
I climbed all day, with the dust eating holes
in my coat and choking me, and the rock cooking me.
What I found was a couple of flat stones
marked up as if the mountain had written all over them.
I was up there a week, working to cool them,
hungry and sweating and unable to make sense of them,
and I fell coming down and broke both of them.
Topping it all, I found everybody down there drooling
over Aaron's cheap figures, and Aaron chortling.

I went up again to get new stones,
and the voices took after me that time and threw me
up between the rocks and said I could see them.
They were right. I could see them. I was standing right behind them,
and I saw them. I saw the mask's insides,
and what I saw is what I have always seen.

I saw the fire, and it flowed, and it was moving away
and not up into me. I saw *nothing,*
and it was widening all the way around me.
I collected two flat stones, and I cut them
so they said what it seemed to me two stones
should say, and I brought them down without dropping them.

The blisters must have doubled my size, and Aaron said
I almost glowed in the dark when I got down.
Even so, it seemed I was pulling my stunts
more often then than down in Egypt. I had to,
to hold them. They had to be led to new land,
and all of them full of crackpot proverbs and cockeyed
ideas about directions. Aaron and I
outbellowed them day after day, and in spite of it
they died. Some of weakness, certainly, but so many of them
died of being strong. The children stood up to it
best, out of knowing no different—but with no
idea what to do with a ploughshare, no
idea what a river is. What could they do
if they got there? What can they even know how to wish for?
I promised them pasture, apple trees, cedar,
waterfalls, snow in the hills, sweetwater
wells instead of these arroyos, wild grapes....

Words. And whatever way I say them, words only.
I no longer know why I say them, even though
the children like hearing them. They come when I call them,
and their eyes are bright, but the light in them is empty.
It is too clear. It contains ... the clarity only.
But they come when I call to them. Once I used to sing them
a song about an eagle and a stone, and each time
I sang it, somehow the song seemed changed,
and the words drifted into the sunlight. I do not
remember the song now, but I remember
that I sang it, and the song was the law, and the law
was the song. The law is a song, I am certain....
And I climbed to the head of this canyon. They said
I could look down at the new land
if I sat here, and I think it is so, but my eyes
are no longer strong, and I am tired now of looking.

from "The Old in Their Knowing"

Herakleitos

1

Herakleitos says a dry soul is wisest and best.
Herakleitos is undeniably
right in these matters. These
bright tatters of wisdom, cast
over grey welter and spume should at any rate yield
a few visions and reflections, a little light
cutting crosswise like a fin,
splayed against the sea's grain
or annealed on the wave crest.

A dry soul. Dry: that is to say
kiln-dried, cured like good lumber or old Bordeaux,
salt-pork and pemmican, meat of the soul
under the chokecherry,
                                        sunlight
and sea salt arrayed in the grain.

2

Herakleitos says something of concord—not
like a carpenter's clamp or lashed
logs, as in Homer.
Harmony with an arched back,
laminated ash upended like an unlaid keel, the curl
of live flesh in the fire, flexed
like the soul between the muscle and the bone, like
the bow, like the lyre.

3

All things are exchangeable for fire and fire for all things,
like gold for goods and goods for gold,
or so sings old
                    Herakleitos.

4

Dead men are gods; men are dead gods, said
Herakleitos. Immortals are mortal, mortals immortal.
The birth of the one is the death of the other;
the dying of one gives life to the other.

The living are dying. The dead live forever,
except when the living disturb them, and this
they must do. The gods die
when men live forever. Air, earth and fire
die too. Dying, we mother and sire

the other: our only and own
incarnation.

5

Wind stirs his ashes.

from the sequence, "*The Book of Silences*" *

II Parśvanatha

What is whole has no face. What
is apart from the whole has no body.

Yet somehow it is, and it is
manysided. Somehow it isn't
and is manysided. Somehow
it is manysided and isn't
and is. It cannot be touched
by the mind or by language, but somehow,
in spite of our thinking and talking,
it is, and in spite of our thinking
and talking, it isn't. Beyond
all our thinking and talking,
it isn't and is. This
is a map of our knowing. Own
nothing. Like breath in your lungs,

the truth passes through you.
Where space, motion and rest
come together is being. Where being
is tainted by death, you find
matter. Like water through cloth,
the unbroken plasma of action
drains through your bones.
What you are will be spelled by whatever
lies trapped in your hand.

On the fenceposts, the weathering heads of your brothers
are thinking of nothing. And speechless. And singing.

III Nagarjuna

What is is swollen like a ripe
fruit, hollow like a cave.
What you touch, hear, taste, see, smell
is the inner perfection of vision.

What reaches into our eyes and our ears
is what is, and that is the wordless, inaudible
song and the brooding, unmusical
speech of the world.

This too
is just one
more opinion
to move through.

What is is what lies
out of sight, thought and talking.
Open them. Open the three
fists clinging to the world.

Open this too.
All positions
are prisons.
No truth is true.

No instruction is certain, no knowledge complete.
If I speak for the serpent, the serpent
may speak for the bird. My position
is that I have no position.

This too.
All fictions
are true,
all intentions,

positions,
and all dispositions
are prisons;
this too.

What is has no essence.
What is is interdependent and empty.
What is is unsingle, undouble, unplural, unborn,
unenduring, unbearing, undying;

what is has no past and no future, no shape
and no nature, no being, no having been, going
to be or becoming, no wholeness and no
incompleteness, no fingers....

This too.
This too
is just one
more opinion.

Outside the perfection of light there is no
total darkness. What causes what is is the hunger
to be and keep being. What is is on loan
from what isn't and its reflection.

What is is on loan from what isn't and is
its disguise. There is no rock bottom.
No centre, no sides, no top and no bottom.
This too.

There are no literal statements.
There is no unmetaphorical language.
This too.
Emptiness also is empty.

Nothing is not nothing. Nothing
is, and *is* is nothing. All that is
is nothing, yet there is
no nothing there that we can cling to.

We are also then
the nothing,
and the nothing
is the hunger,

and the hunger
is the question
and the answer:
be pure wonder.

V Sengzho

The thought of the gods is dark water. The gods
have their destinies too as they move through the world.
Our speech does not reach them. As for our speechlessness,
what shall we say? And to whom shall we say it?
What is is not easy and graceful to speak of.
My teacher, a foreigner, lame in the tongue
like a caged raven, knew this.
I, however, was born here. Forgive me,
that sometimes I sink into elegant phrase.

The gods' minds and their mindprints are one
and the same. With us it is different. Our footprints
fall off as we walk through the world. Our brilliant
assertions tack like October leaves
through the air before mouldering. Yes and no
are at home in each other, not elsewhere. What is
and who knows of its presence are one and the same.

The feet are the link
between earth and the body. Begin there.
The lungs are the link between body and air.
The hands, these uprooted feet, are the means
of our shaping and grasping. Clasp them.
The eyes are the hands of the head;
its feet are the ears.

We are all of us here in the hidden
house of the unnamed. You
who insist we must visit
and name it have ceased to be there.

X Han Shan

Friends, the mind, or at any rate
my mind at this moment, is much
like the moon. It is swollen
with light, it is dry and in motion.

Its taste and its smell, its feel
in the skull, are those of the moon
over the steep hills and the bottomless
pools of deep autumn.

Friends, what is is much like the pool.
What is not is not unlike the air,
and what neither is nor is not neither is
nor is not like or unlike the hills.

This being so, there is no
comparison, is no description, assertion,
negation. I tell you conclusively,
there can be no conclusions.

I am leaving now. Please,
no applause. Those who know how to live
will leave with me
in different directions.

XIV Yunmen Wenyan

Stones and trees are my teachers, but
there are others. The truth of the world
sparkles in slopbuckets, toilet bowls, turds,
and in festering sores.

Are your eyes plugged up with light,
your ears plugged up with music
and your nose with sweet spring air?
Everything that has ever existed is medicine.

Bright emptiness burns in the doorway.
In the cupboard it fills up the dishes and bowls.
The flames in the stove are reciting the law.
Past, present and future have come here to listen.

**Parśvanatha* (c. 820-776 B.C.?) A North Indian sage, traditionally counted the 23rd patriarch of the Jains.*

Nagarjuna (2nd. century A.D.?) "The White Serpent." A dialectical philosopher who taught near Amarvati, on the Krishna River, in Andhra Pradesh.

Sengzhao (Seng-chao, 384-414) A Buddhist philosopher born in Shaanxi. He studied at Chang'an with the captive translator Kumarajiva.

Han Shan (fl. c. 800 AD) The hermit poet of Cold Mountain in the Tiantai Range, Zhejiang.

Yunmen Wenyan (Yun-men Wen-yen, 864-949) A Zen teacher born near Shangai. He taught in northern Guangdong.

from the sequence *"Lyell Island Variations"*

II Thin Man Washing

...et la terre mauvaise dans le champ de son cœur
René Char

Once upon a time there was a man
who never hungered anymore,
or so I heard—he had devoured so many legacies,
bitten off anything, eaten through anyone who came near—

who one day found
that his table was cleared,
his bed emptied, his children renamed,
and the soil gone sour in the uplands of his heart.

He had dug no grave; he had thought to survive.
He had nothing to give; he had less to receive.
Objects avoided him, animals lied to him,
the Diamond Sutra hung, untranslatable, on his wall.

It was only then that he crept back in
and stole hunger and shaped it into
a bowl, in which, to this day, when no one
is looking, and the wind isn't blowing, he bathes.

Sunday Morning

for Don McKay & Jan Zwicky

Moonset at sunrise, the mind
dividing between them. The teeth
of the young sun sink through the breast of the cloud.
And a great white pelican rests in the bay,
on his way from Great Slave Lake
to Guatemala.
The mind is made out of the animals
it has attended.
In all the unspoken languages,
it is their names.
Mule deer, black bear, killer whale, salmon.

To know means to hold no opinions: to know
meaning thinks, thinking means.
The mind is the place not already taken.
The mind is not-yet-gathered beads of water
in the teeth of certain leaves—
Saxifraga punctata, close by the stream
under the ridge leading south to Mount Hozameen,
for example—and the changing answers of the moon.
The mind is light rain gathered
on the ice-scarred rock, a crumpled mirror.

To be is to speak with the bristlecone
pines and the whitebarks,
glaciers and rivers, grasses and schists,
and if it is permitted, once also
with pelicans. Being
is what there is room for in that
conversation. The loved is what stays
in the mind; that is, it has meaning,
and meaning keeps going, This
is the definition of meaning.

What is is not speech.
What is is the line
between the unspeakable
and the already spoken.

Robert Bringhurst
In Praise of Vacant Lots

My experience, as a simple pagan, is this: if you listen to the forest, if you listen to the mountains, if you listen to the snow, a lot of spiritual arthritis disappears; a lot of crutches fall away. The religions—capitalism, Christianity, Marxism, nationalism, Islam and many others—all dissolve, leaving the fossilized and badly eroded myths of which they are made. The mountains are the mind. But if you cut the forest down, your mind will disappear and in its place there will be shopping malls and churches and TV. If you mistake them for the world, you will think that you are thinking, but the truth is, you will think what you are told.

Strong sensations, Plato says, are like rivets or nails that fasten the soul to the body. He goads old Socrates to say we should avoid pains and pleasures whenever we can, so the soul can more easily leave the body behind. I like the metaphor. I don't like the advice. Zuoqiu Ming, who lived in Plato's time but in a different place—at Luoyang in northern Henan—makes one of his own historically fictional characters say:

When spiritual beings have a place to return to, they need not become malicious. I have allowed them a place to return to.

Zuoqiu Ming's implied advice provides a good and simple rationale for wilderness areas, national parks, Japanese gardens, fallow fields, vacant lots and other sources of salvation—and for string quartets and temples, poems and paintings too, if they are good enough to mix with alpine meadows, rocks and trees.

Zuoqiu Ming has been interpreted to mean that you can cover the earth with factories, and chop the rivers up with dams, so long as you build a few cathedrals, parks or temples in between. But picnic sites and sonnets and cathedrals are no adequate apology or substitute for the watersheds and forests that cathedral-building cultures, and temple-building cultures, and great-hall-of-the-people-building cultures have destroyed. Is it possible that, if the government of China thought a little more about the thought of Zuoqiu Ming and the poetry of Lao Zi, it would never have invaded and plundered Tibet nor ordered its troops to shoot the students in Tian'anmen Square? If politicians and businessmen could openly admit that spirits live in the rocks and trees and lakes and rivers, could we also stop assassinating the planet that keeps us alive?

Plato leans on the Presocratics, yet he departs from his tradition just as radically as Mao Zedong from his. The gods, who are allowed a rich emotional and physical life in Homer's poems, are sentenced in Plato's prose to pure abstraction. It is beautiful prose, of course, and it is beautiful abstraction. Plato, even more than Mao or Marx, was a gifted writer, seducing himself as well as his readers, page after page. But the beauty of a sentence, like the beauty of a face, is not a guarantee that wisdom lives inside.

Pure abstraction has captivating charms, like pure carnality. But I am happiest, I think, when I can somehow sense the spirit in the flesh, the flesh in the spirit, the song in the mouth, the breath in the song, the nerves and tendons in the thought, the thought in the marrow of the bone. I like to taste the cake as well as think it through. The body rots when the spirit is gone. I think the spirit ought to rot—and I think that it does, though I don't know how fast or how slowly—when it cannot reenter the body.

When spirit does invest the flesh, and when we sense that it belongs there, the division between secular and sacred disappears. The nails of perception hold the whole together—just as Herakleitos and the Haida poet Ghandl, and a lot of other wise men and women who are missing from the canon, said perceptions ought to do.

I have another hunch. It is that societies like ours, which produce huge piles of spiritless matter—trash and scrap and useless new consumer "goods"—must be evicting spirits from their houses at roughly the same rate: producing hordes of disembodied and invisible refugees. I often think I hear their cries.

When they are made out of honesty and need, affection and attention, the things we make are usually real. Barns, bricks, poems, boats, shoes, acts of love, and loaves of genuine bread. The things we make that way are homes for spirits. Things we make from greed instead of need—like television sets and advertising jingles and fast food—give shelter only to demons, if indeed they shelter anything at all. Demons can be trained, its seems, to do a lot of tasks. But demons are like viruses; they use us to reproduce themselves. They are the parasites, if you like, of the spiritual world. These days, in the cities, there seem to be a lot of them around. An epidemic, you could say—and not one we could solve by taking pills or burning witches.

Leonard Cohen

Poet, novelist, singer, songwriter/composer, and recording artist, LEONARD COHEN was born in Montreal in 1934. He has produced an impressive body of work including nine volumes of poetry and two novels. His selected poems, *Stranger Music: Selected Poems and Songs* (McClelland & Stewart and Leonard Cohen Stranger Music) appeared in 1993. In 1991, he was made an Officer of the Order of Canada. He has received three Juno Awards, and was one of six recipients of the 1993 Governor General's Performing Arts Awards for lifetime achievement. He is an Officer of the Order of Canada and an inductee into the Juno Hall of Fame (1991). Mr. Cohen is currently living in Los Angeles.

Gift

You tell me that silence
is nearer to peace than poems
but if for my gift
I brought you silence
(for I know silence)
you would say
This is not silence
this is another poem
and you would hand it back to me.

from *Beautiful Losers*

What Is a Saint

What is a saint? A saint is someone who has achieved a remote human possibility. It is impossible to say what that possibility is. I think it has something to do with the energy of love. Contact with this energy results in the exercise of a kind of balance in the chaos of existence. A saint does not dissolve the chaos; if he did the world would have changed long ago. I do not think that a saint dissolves the chaos even for himself, for there is something arrogant and warlike in the notion of a man setting the universe in order. It is a kind of balance that is his glory. He rides the drifts like an escaped ski. His course is a caress of the hill. His track is a drawing of the snow in a moment of its particular arrangement with wind and rock. Something in him so loves the world that he gives himself to the laws of gravity and chance. Far from flying with the angels, he traces with the fidelity of a seismograph needle the state of the solid bloody landscape. His house is dangerous and finite, but he is at home in the world. He can love the shapes of human beings, the fine and twisted shapes of the heart. It is good to have among us such men, such balancing monsters of love.

Roshi

Roshi poured me a glass of Courvoisier. We were in the cabin on Mt. Baldy, summer of 1977. We were listening to the crickets.

— Kone, Rossi said, you should write cricket poem.

— I've already written a cricket poem. It was in this cabin two years ago.

— Oh.

Roshi fried some sliced pork in sunflower oil and boiled a three-minute noodle soup. We finished one bottle of Courvoisier and opened another.

— Yah, Kone, you should write cricket poem.

— That is a very Japanese idea, Roshi.

— So.

We listened to the crickets a while longer. Then we closed the light so we could open the door and get the breeze without the flies coming in.

— Yah. Cricket.

— Roshi, give me your idea of a cricket poem.

— Ha, ha. Okay:

dark night (said Roshi)
cricket sound break out
cricket girlfriend listening

— That's pretty good, Roshi.

— dark night (Roshi began again)
walking on the path
suddenly break out cricket sound
where is my lover?

— I don't like that one.

— cricket! cricket! (Roshi cried)
you are my lover
now I am walking path by alone
but I am not lonely with you

— I'm afraid not, Roshi. The first one was good.

Then the crickets stopped for a while and Roshi poured the Courvoisier into our glasses. It was a peaceful night.

— Yah, Kone, said Roshi very softly. You should write more sad.

from *The Book of Mercy* (four poems)

I Stopped to Listen

I stopped to listen, but he did not come. I began again with a sense of loss. As this sense deepened I heard him again. I stopped stopping and I stopped starting, and I allowed myself to be crushed by ignorance. This was a strategy, and didn't work at all. Much time, years were wasted in such a minor mode. I bargain now. I offer buttons for his love. I beg for mercy. Slowly he yields. Haltingly he moves toward his throne. Reluctantly the angels grant to one another permission to sing. In a transition so delicate it cannot be marked, the court is established on beams of golden symmetry, and once again I am a singer in the lower choirs, born fifty years ago to raise my voice this high, and no higher.

The Eyes of Men

In the eyes of men he falls, and in his own eyes too. He falls from his high place, he trips on his achievement. He falls to you, he falls to know you. It is sad, they say. See his disgrace, say the ones at his heel. But he falls radiantly toward the light to which he falls. They cannot see who lifts him as he falls, or how his falling changes, and he himself bewildered till his heart cries out to bless the one who holds him in his falling. And in his fall he hears his heart cry out, his heart explains why he is falling, why he had to fall, and he gives over to the fall. Blessed are you, clasp of the falling. He falls into the sky, he falls into the light, none can hurt him as he falls. Blessed are you, shield of the falling. Wrapped in his fall, concealed within his fall, he finds the place, he is gathered in. While his hair streams back and his clothes tear in the wind, he is held up, comforted, he enters into the place of his fall. Blessed are you, embrace of the falling, foundation of the light, master of the human accident.

You Who Pour Mercy Into Hell

You who pour mercy into hell, sole authority in highest and the lowest worlds, let your anger disperse the mist in this aimless place, where even my sins fall short of the mark. Let me be with you again, absolute companion, let me study your ways which are just beyond the hope of evil. Seize my heart out of its fantasy, direct my heart from the fiction of secrecy, you who know the secrets of every heart, whose mercy is to be the secret of longing. Let every heart declare its secret, let every song disclose your love, let us bring to you the sorrows of our freedom. Blessed are you, who opens a gate, in every moment, to enter in truth or tarry in hell. Let me be with you again, let me put this away, you who wait beside me, who have broken down your world to gather hearts. Blessed is your name, blessed is the confession of your name. Kindle the darkness of my calling, let me cry to the one who judges the heart in justice and mercy. Arouse my heart again with the limitless breath you breathe into me, arouse the secret from obscurity.

All My Life

All my life is broken unto you, and all my glory soiled unto you. Do not let the spark of my soul go out in the even sadness. Let me raise the brokenness to you, to the world where the breaking is for love. Do not let the words be mine but change them into truth. With these lips instruct my heart, and let fall into the world what is broken in the world. Lift me up to the wrestling of faith. Do not leave me where the sparks go out, and the jokes are told in the dark, and new things are called forth and appraised in the scale of the terror. Face me to the rays of love, O source of light, or face me to the majesty of your darkness, but not here, do not leave me here, where death is forgotten, and the new thing grins.

If It Be Your Will

If it be your will
that I speak no more,
and my voice be still
as it was before;
I will speak no more,
I shall abide until
I am spoken for,
if it be your will.

If it be your will
that a voice be true,
from this broken hill
I will sing to you.
From this broken hill
all your praises they shall ring
if it be your will
to let me sing.

If it be your will,
if there is a choice,
let the rivers fill,
let the hills rejoice.
Let your mercy spill
on all these burning hearts in hell,
if it be your will
to make us well.

And draw us near
and bind us tight,
all your children here
in their rags of light;
in our rags of light,
all dressed to kill;
and end this night,
if it be your will.

LEONARD COHEN

Anthem

The birds they sang
at the break of day
Start again,
I heard them say,
Don't dwell on what
has passed away
or what is yet to be.

The wars they will
be fought again
The holy dove
be caught again
bought and sold and bought again;
the dove is never free.

Ring the bells that still can ring.
Forget your perfect offering.
There is a crack in everything.
That's how the light gets in.

We asked for signs
the signs were sent:
the birth betrayed,
the marriage spent;
the widowhood
of every government—
signs for all to see.

Can't run no more
with that lawless crowd
while the killers in high places
say their prayers out loud.
But they've summoned up
a thundercloud
They're going to hear from me.

Ring the bells that still can ring
Forget your perfect offering.
There is a crack in everything.
That's how the light gets in.

You can add up the parts
but you won't have the sum
You can strike up the march,
there is no drum.
Every heart
to love will come
but like a refugee.

Ring the bells that still can ring
Forget your perfect offering.
There is a crack in everything.
That's how the light gets in.

A Deep Happiness

A deep happiness
has seized me
My Christian friends say
that I have received
the Holy Spirit
It is only the truth of solitude
It is only the torn anemone
fastened to the rock
its root exposed
to the off-shore wind
O friend of my scribbled life
your heart is like mine—
your loneliness
will bring you home

Hydra, 1981

Lorna Crozier

LORNA CROZIER was born in Swift Current, Saskatchewan in 1948. A series of poems, which became part of the book *Angels of Flesh, Angels of Silence,* won first prize for poetry in the CBC Radio Literary Competition in 1987. Her eighth book of poetry, *Inventing the Hawk,* received the Governor General's Award in 1992, the Pat Lowther Award for the Best Book of Poetry by a Canadian Woman, and the Canadian Authors' Association Award for poetry. *Everything Arrives at the Light* received the Pat Lowther Award for 1995, and a selection of poems from the book was awarded the National Magazine Gold Medal. She has held several writer-in-residence positions, most recently at the University of Toronto. With poet Patrick Lane, she lives on Vancouver Island where she teaches in the Department of Creative Writing at the University of Victoria. Her latest two books, *A Saving Grace: The Collected Poems of Mrs. Bentley* and *The Transparency of Grief,* the winner of (M)Other Tongue Press's chapbook competition, were published in 1996.

Myths

There is a story of a swan.
See the birthmark on the back of my neck
under my hair. That is where the great bird
pinched me in her beak, snatching me from the sea
and carrying my wet, salty body to the shore.
This is a story I could believe.
Sometimes the wings of a bird beat against
my skull. Feathers fill my mouth and eyes
with a whiteness like winter.

Or I was carried on a dolphin's back.
She pushed me to shore with her soft nose
then turned and disappeared under the waves,
the notes of her song hovering above the water.
In the blue light of evening, alone in the house,
I float through rooms, my sides sleek and slippery.

I was not made from a thin, dry rib
white and bare as if chewed and sucked
by a small dog. These breasts did not come
from a man's side, this round belly, this
hollow at the centre. We dreamed each other
at the same time and we dreamed a garden.
When we awoke there was wind in the leaves
above us apples glowing like red moons
as we turned to one another in the sweet green air.

Angel of Infinity

When she first touched the angel
her fingers burned
though the angel was invisible,
so much time and space,
so much light. The second time

the angel took shape
under the apple tree. The cat
watched the wings
surprise the air,
each feather so pure and well defined
the woman tried to count them
to keep her mind on something real.

What do you ask of the Angel
of Infinity?
More room for your children, more
time, more time.

The cat seemed undisturbed.
He bunted his head
against the angel's legs
as if this were an ordinary guest
with cats of her own
in whatever house she lived in.

The woman felt comfort in this
and in seeing the wind
that lifted her hair
move the angel's feathers
so the air was filled with rustling
softer than the stir of leaves.

Maybe that was the blessing;
the cat purring in the shadow
of the angel's wings,
the apples on fire
in their usual way
in the apple tree

the wind
                    touching everything
at the same time

On the Seventh Day

On the first day God said
Let there be light.
And there was light.
On the second day
God said, *Let there be light,*
and there was more light.

What are you doing? asked God's wife,
knowing he was the dreamy sort.
You created light yesterday.

I forgot, God said. *What can I do
about it now?*

Nothing, said his wife.
But pay attention!
And in a huff she left
to do the many chores
a wife must do in the vast
though dustless rooms of heaven.

On the third day God said
Let there be light. And
on the fourth and fifth
(his wife off visiting his mother).

When she returned there was only
the sixth day left. The light
was so blinding, so dazzling
God had to stretch and stretch the sky to hold it
and the sky took up all the room—
it was bigger than anything
even God could imagine.
Quick, his wife said,
make something to stand on!
God cried, *Let there be earth!*
and a thin line of soil
nudged against the sky like a run-over snake
bearing all the blue in the world on its back.

On the seventh day God rested
as he always did. Well, *rest*
wasn't exactly the right word,
his wife had to admit.
On the seventh day God
went into his study
and wrote in his journal
in huge curlicues and loops
and large crosses on the *t's,*
changing all the facts, of course,
even creating Woman
from a Man's rib, imagine that!
But why be upset? she thought.
Who's going to believe it?

Anyway, she had her work to do.
Everything he'd forgotten
she had to create
with only a day left to do it.
Leaf by leaf,
paw by paw, two by two,
and now nothing
could be immortal
as in the original plan.

Go out and multiply, yes,
she'd have to say it,
but there was too little room
for life without end,
forever and ever,
on that thin spit of earth
under that huge prairie sky.

Inventing the Hawk

She didn't believe the words
when she first heard them, that blue
bodiless sound entering her ear.
But now something was in the air,
a sense of waiting as if
the hawk itself were there
just beyond the light, blinded
by a fine-stitched leather hood
she must take apart with her fingers.
Already she had its voice,
the scream that rose from her belly
echoed in the dark inverted
canyon of her skull.

She built its wings, feather by feather,
the russet smoothness of its head,
the bead-bright eyes,
in that moment between sleep and waking.

Was she the only one
who could remember them,
who knew their shape and colours, the way
they could tilt the world with a list of wings?
Perhaps it was her reason for living
so long in this hard place
of wind and sky, the stunted trees
reciting their litany of loss
outside her window.

Elsewhere surely someone was drawing
gophers and mice out of the air.
Maybe that was also her job,
so clearly she could see them.
She'd have to lie here forever,
dreaming hair after hair,
summoning the paws (her own heart
turning timid, her nostrils twitching).

Then she would cause the seeds
in their endless variety—the ones
floating light as breath,
the ones with burrs and spears
that caught in her socks
when she was a child,
the radiant, uninvented blades of grass.

The Language of Angels

Their marvellous mouths say nothing,
say nothing. What you hear is
their silence. It falls through the seven
celestial spheres, gathers in the dark
behind the rock they rolled from the tomb.
Here their wings translate the air.
Their feet, more beautiful than any Homer knew,
interpret each blade of grass,
an exegesis of the earth. Words,
thoughts, senses are all one body,
the body before you that burns.
All flesh these
words, these extravagant mouths,
mute as swans.

Naming the Light

Naming the light as the Inuit
the snow. The light around my father's

hands as he lay dying, his worn
fingers curled. Unborn animals, sleeping.

Womb-light and the glow of dreams,
they slow you down like water.

My father's body flew up in smoke,
ashes under my nails. Ten moons

rose from my fingers above the lake
where we scattered him,

the shore luminous with alkali
and lichen-splattered stones.

His brief shining in the air
I hold to me now in this place

where winter nights are darkest
because there is no snow.

The Souls of Animals

> *Having no souls, they have come,*
> *Anyway, beyond their knowing.*
> —James Dickey, "*The Heaven of Animals*"

If animals have no souls
it's because they do not need them.
There is something forever about their time
on earth, whether they move on wing, paw or hoof,
or slide with huge, cold bodies
across the blue-green worlds.

Wherever they dwell, their gaze
when they look at you
comes from a great height—
the yellow of hawk and panther eye—
or so close up
they've slipped under the leaves
of your eyelids and stare from the inside out.

In books of the dead the human soul
becomes bird or butterfly
or soft-pawed, graceful thing.
Grant animals a soul: might it not leave
their bodies in the shape of ours?
Assume the best of us, the high forehead,
the shapely arms, the exactitude of
thumb on index finger.

That's what those bright ones are,
those people we glimpse with a glow about them,
an ecstasy. The souls of animals
crossing from one country to another,
pausing for a moment among us
only to rise in glory,
beasts again.

Noah's Wife

Of all the animals it was the snails
I loved best. There was beauty in the others,
the foxes' flaming tails, the eyes
of owls, pools of pure light
where I would have bathed if not
for all the water lapping,
my mind an island of eroding sand.

The salamanders, too, with their grace.
Their fingers seemed to stroke green
music from the air. Cats were my familiars,
perhaps too close for me
to remember my earthly delight
in the small hairs inside their ears
like the ones that guided bees into
the foxglove blooms drowning in my garden.

After a week at sea the air smelled
of rotting pomegranate and banana,
the autumn scent of hay, waste that grew
on wooden planks like strange
misshapen mushrooms slick with flies.

When I watched from the deck
almost all I had loved swept away,
it was not my husband
but the snails who comforted me. Each
came aboard with its house intact,
its room devoid of altars, of reminiscence,
the small things a boy might save
to remind him of the earth.

Like a woman the snail tucked itself
inside its shadow, slid on silence,
whatever it said to its mate no one could hear
nor the cries when they came together
on the underside of leaves.

As the ark sailed on my strange imagining,
and dove after dove fell from the sky,
I built my shell: one door, one window, stairs
leading nowhere because there'd been no stars
for days. Rain hammered the waves,
shattered the faces that stared at me
with the eyes of dolphins.
I began to see my husband's penis
as a snail's silver horn. Without words
I welcomed it under the eye of his angry god
whose spittle had drowned the world.

When my husband slept I slipped into
my own domed emptiness
and for no reason I could understand,
I licked the snails one by one
and placed them on his eyelids,
living coins.

from *A Saving Grace: The Collected Poems of Mrs. Bentley*

Country Dweller

Paul, the school teacher
who drops by to see us
now and then, tells me
pagan means *country dweller*—
that's where we've gone wrong.
We've tried to tame the wild gods
and make them one.

Maybe even Philip
could believe in them.
A horse god. Among the reeds
and rushes, a wind god.
In aspen leaves, a god of light.

The smallest, the most slender
is the god of rain.

I tell Paul she must be
female, a four-legged animal
with soft paws and swishing tail
for that's what we hear
when she comes near us
for her green communion
with the grass.

Wilderness

Like Mrs. Moodie I could say
the wilderness moved inside me
but where there is no bush,
the wilderness is different.

It's really space that rushes at you
in spite of fences, the grid roads
laid in graphs across the earth.

A space not as empty as
you might imagine, it's a thing itself
minus details you can't separate
the whole into any parts.
The worst is

                              it doesn't need you.
It goes on and on whether the land
is broken or not, whether a town makes
its small exclamation mark or flattens out.

What's most like the prairie
is the mind of God, the huge way
he must have of looking at the world.
That's why I feel small and scared
inside myself, and yet at times
full of wonder.

LORNA CROZIER
TWO GOLDFISH IN THE SNOW

This winter a freak snow storm hit the West Coast. Before the worst of it, when we couldn't make it through the back yard, the snow waist-high, we walked to the pond to check on the goldfish. Two of them lay embedded in a thin skin of ice. Patrick broke through to scoop them out and laid them on the snow at the edge of the pond while we tried to see the others. Alive, they drifted in the cold viscous water as if suspended between two elements like someone dreaming. I looked back at the two dead fish, so orange against the white. Their presence seemed magnified, weighted with significance. Part of their power was the startling beauty of paradox—against the snow, two gleaming fish the size and colour of candle flames broken from a wick. No matter how long I gazed, I couldn't figure out what it was they meant though they were charged with meaning. They remained unreadable like glyphs from a language not my own, yet they were simply two dead fish placed for a moment in the snow.

This is one place where poetry begins, at the edge of the ineffable, the silent site where words dissolve and one's understanding has more to do with intuition than reasoning, with emotion than logic. What cannot be named is the proper subject of poetry, even though poems are populated with the concrete and commonplace: an old stove, lichen on a stone, an egg carton, a cat's whisker. How can poetry not include the spiritual when even these familiar things are endowed with a presence as forceful as the objects our official religions have sanctified? They resonate with an energy we try to put words to, and yet they remain irrefutably and blessedly themselves.

In poems I admire, the poets who personify, who don't sacrifice the essence of the thing for the sake of the comparison, but to use Galway Kinnell's words, they animalize, vegetablize and mineralize themselves. If we could do this, on a daily basis, how differently we would see the world and our place in it! Anytime I've experienced what I would call "the spiritual," the boundaries between me and the Other break down. It's as if someone erases my human outline, pressed into paper with such a thick, hard stroke, so that I can suddenly reach across what separates my species from the rest, and briefly, wonderfully, connect.

Sometimes that connection leads to words and to visions of angels, by which I mean the spark of the spiritual in the everyday world around me. Sometimes I'm led back to the Judeo-Christian stories central to my childhood in an attempt to honour what they have often omitted, including the sacredness of the female and the body, that bountiful angel of flesh. But there are moments, too, when speaking seems impossible and, at least for a time, inappropriate. Even when the words are found and transcribed into poetry, they reflect that near-miss, that muteness, the object's refusal of language. The quotidian remains as stubbornly untranslatable as two goldfish lying in the snow in my backyard. Falling now for days in this usually immutable green world, on the cedars, the rhododendrons, and the verbena about to blossom, snow silences everything it touches though it melts without pause on our tongues.

Barry Dempster

BARRY DEMPSTER was born in Scarborough, Ontario, in 1952. He was educated in psychology, working for many years as part of a crisis team at the Queen Street Mental Health Centre in Toronto. His first book of poetry, *Fables for Isolated Men* (Guernica, 1982), was a finalist for the 1982 Governor General's Award. Around this same time, he became involved with *Poetry Canada*, serving as Reviews Editor for over a decade; he was also Poetry Editor from 1989-1996. Dempster has published six more volumes of poetry, including *The Unavoidable Man* (Quarry, 1990), *Letters from a Long Illness with the World, the D.H. Lawrence Poems* (Brick, 1993) and *Fire and Brimstone* (Empyreal Press, 1997). He is also the author of a children's book, *David and the Daydreams* (Guernica), two collections of short stories, *Real Places and Imaginary Men* and *Writing Home* (both Oberon), and a novel, *The Ascension of Jesse Rapture* (Quarry). He won *Arc*'s Confederation Poets' Prize in 1995 and was recently the recipient of a Scarborough Bi-Centennial Award of Merit. Presently, he lives in Holland Landing, Ontario, on the edge of the Holland Marsh, with his wife, Karen, and their three cats.

Souls

Countries rest upon a pair
of praying hands, pieces of
the soul supporting lands.
Hindus holding the Ganges
like a shore, Muslims scaling
Mecca heights, Buddhists shaping
futures with their daily plans.

Christians lift the land on
broken backs, a ladder of
cross and nails. Looming from
steeples, a saviour tree,
a brilliant body wide with arms,
a pose of constant embrace.

Let us all strive to be more
like our souls. Hindus gathering
together in a giant sea,
Muslims with piercing eyes, Buddhists
opening their endless minds.

Let us stand as tall
as beams of wood, and if we fall
let it be upon our knees.

Let us hang upon a door, bear up
our dark responsibilities.

Let us forgive ourselves
the sadness of standing
so alone, believe in
the possibilities of God.

Everywhere people press against
the walls of churches, temples,
synagogues, arms and legs outstretched.

BARRY DEMPSTER

They are praying to the living shores
the perfect heights.

They are holding the world in place.

Angels and Poems

Two in the morning, an angel
holds me by the wrist.
Is she teaching me to fly?
Am I baffled in a dream?

Awake, my hand is empty,
windows sealed shut. Only snow
playing tricks with diamond eyes.

Eerie how the night will lead a man
to live an impossible life.
This ordinary hand
miraculous in the mind.

Somewhere in sleep an angel
reaches for my wrist. Fingers fly.

I am not angelic though, too much
a chilly breeze, a lumpy bed.

At best, an arm poking
out from drifts of snow.

Awake, I think of poetry,
a place for putting dreams.
An angel perches boldly
on the page, bright, untamed,
like a green canary.

Imagination made whole.
Pretending to fly by simply
saying so. The night poised
over paper, a self-styled wing.

Look, emptiness. Look, diamond
eyes. My wrist wears poems and soars.

In Search of Mary

I come to churches in search of
Mary, through basement corridors
of melba toast and lukewarm wine.

A Protestant, there are
no marble thighs to press
my cheek against, no stained
glass robes shimmering at
the throat, no prayers as full-
bodied as a woman.

I will try to believe in
faith—finger shadows on the bare
walls, the shapes of draped coats
in the hall, an occasional
soprano in the choir.

Mary, what is man if not
a child playing with
his fingers in the light?

A boy burrows in the closet
in his mother's coat, seeking
the shape of an arm or breast.
Later, sleepy stories, saying
prayers, the child waits awake,
a perfect stillness curved and clear.

I will hold you, Mary,
a body beneath my tongue.
Desire, the size of a church.

Searching Mary everywhere
down church corridors,
in lukewarm shimmerings of wine.

I will peer through open fingers,
white walls marbled in the sun.
Will drape a coat across my arm,
the weight of a woman's hand.
Create my own full-bodied
prayers, all curves, so clear, a voice
burrowed deep in perfect words.

Mary, what is man if not
the shadow of his faith?

Adam and Innocence

In the beginning Adam was naive.
Playing names, fussing with
the breeze, pretending to be
a lion or a rock. Whatever
pleased. For God's keen eye
he hung from lower branches
in the shape and dangle of a fruit.
Posed naked on a cliff, a model

moon. The first experiment:
will he devise a language, be
seasonal, will he sink or swim?
Give of himself for the sake of
loneliness? He sat on the cold
hard ground and listened to
the sounds of everything. When
he spoke to streams, he believed
in their memory. Darkness
nothing more than a concealed face.

It is important for children
to learn to eat with forks, to
know that life is round, no Santa
Claus, the body covered up. I teach
little Adam he is neither an orange
nor Spiderman. Do not speak
to strangers, beware of promises.
A night-light glows in the nursery,
a plastic angel with a pink face.

Adam is always an innocent.
In the beginning children are never
reflections of ourselves. Wish
on a newborn, wish for a keen future.
Rather than die, wouldn't we all
choose to be rocks? Or moon about
the universe, like a bunch of angels
warming themselves on children's eyes.
To watch is a lonely occupation:
the inside wanting out. Adam and I
sit on the bedroom floor and I hear
every single sound he makes. I am
swayed by promises of memory.
The simple face beaming through
the shadows of my disbelief.

from *Letters from a Long Illness with the World: the D.H. Lawrence Poems*

Hampstead 1915

...too much corruption, old age and a terror that sets man against man as if we were all gladiators. The English take to war with an uncommon fury, most of them not even caring to clarify the enemy. I am the enemy with my dirty little books and my abandoned patriotism. I am the enemy whenever I think a new thought. What I would most like to do is transform that newness into something greater than personality: a new spirit, a new life. Creativity, unanimity, rebirth. I will rush into the future and fix it from rolling down that endless hill of time. People don't understand that: reshaping the very essence of life, stopping God in his cold tracks. We have too long believed in weakness; if the Creator truly is, then his main ambition is to blow new life into his creations. Blow away! I have stopped stumbling and collapsing, I am breathing in...

A Million Words...

Vence 1930

Seasons are arranged in a vase
by the window: a veil of violets
dusty daisies, a wrinkled-yellow
chestnut spray. Icicles grow clear
and thin, like magic flutes.

Phosphorus looks down upon us all
a crystal God who knows the shape of
marrow in our bones. Wind is to snap
us, rain to wilt. Sunlight needles.
Fingers digging fast, the ends of
earth, the glowing rock of graves.

What I will miss most about the world
is change. Introspective skies
suddenly catching sight of closed
umbrellas. Real flesh and blood
emerging from the sombre cells of
books. Women revealing their unexpected
selves. Someone else's death.
From this dying hand came the brandishing
of clouds and torches: a dream landscape
where meadows flourished under crops of
birds, spreading into continental shelves.
The birth of an ideal sustains the man
until both become a way of life; death
diminishing nothing but the self.

Years from here a stranger will walk
into my house, *the home of the infamous*
etc..., claiming to feel my spirit
in the antique walls. Only the words
always wanting out.

The world of the dead is a megalopolis.
Shakespeare scrunched beside Wordsworth
who I could swear is almost sitting
on my knee. The combination of us all
will haunt you, the quantity.

I rush too far ahead, the daily world
peeling from my brain like cobweb.
All I seem to care about is living
not the life itself. The taste of water
rather than the soggy map. The sound
of words, touch of body hair, smell of
sea, look of mirrors. I will leave
nothing of myself behind, just these
second-hand sensations never quite complete.

The world is eternal, not the man.
I was something in the air, in the
rosebush: a spot of cold, a thorn.

Field upon field of daisies. Chestnuts
falling like a skyful of wish-wearied
stars. The countryside unconscious
with snow. The world is larger than
an eye or mouth, and death promises
to be fuller than even the greediest of
hands. I do not believe in puny ghosts
but in giant plans: a lifetime that
just might change the way the world
goes on alone.

from *Fire and Brimstone*

Sunday School and the Promised Land

In Sunday school, Christ's hometown
was every colour in a crayon box,
from the strawberry red noses
of the donkeys, to the ink black
winter skies. Israel was the
Promised Land, a temporary title

like Miss America or the Stanley Cup,
before God moved his whole caravan
to North America, destination
the Scarborough Gospel Hall.
The Old Testament
crawled across deserts, through seas,
sprawling breathless in the Bay of Fundy,
bumming a ride to Toronto
in the back of a livestock truck.
The Gentiles pressed their ears
to the chocolate coloured ground
and heard the new centre of the earth.

Matthew, Mark, Luke and John wrote
words white as sheets. They're talking
to you, my Sunday school teacher claimed,
a little boy who felt less solid
than Casper the Friendly Ghost.
From Bethlehem to Golgotha to
a Brethren Hall on Warden Ave.
When Christ was a child like me
he loved to ride the streetcars,
his shoulder-length hair drifting
in the breeze. He sang
his daily God Save the Queen
and hid most of his Christmas cake
in a balled-up serviette.
Every Sunday he memorized psalms,
watching slides of faraway children
better known as heathens; exactly
like me, wondering why God had chosen him
while leaving the rest of the world wild.

Three Prayers

1

Oh valuator, great iris in the sky,
keep me like a cat's-eye, like
a Mickey Mantle or a Rocket Richard,
an English pound or a Portuguese stamp.

Realtor of all my hopes and fears,
treasure me in leather books or
velvet bags, swaddle me with cellophane.

Save me, like the decorative doll
on my mother's showy bed.

2

As it was in the beginning, let
me dally in the divided light.

Hang me from a sunbeam, my
collar ablaze, never let me
swoon from your sight.

Protect me from the charred, the
scorched, that slash of darkness
shrinking the day like a missionary's head.

3

Stain me with the sky dye
of your atomic stare.

Come inside, set phosphorus fires
in my blood, pour radium
in every follicle. Use me,
a bone's unearthly glow.

I am litmus, raiment,
thy will be done.

Scar me with your preciousness,
live me longer than when.

Holy Face

His hands and sleeves held out
like estuaries, reaching for the sea
of me. Jesus looming
from my bedroom wall, dominating
the pirate curtains and kitty
calendar, even the moonlight
that hangs from my closet door. In
the early hours of the morning, His
fingertips inch over hardwood
floors, little drowning pools of light.

Hours alone, just the two of us,
staring. Boldly, I'd pull back the covers
and show Him my bum, something
to shock the nakedness of His baby
fingers, the way the nails
were so translucently pink
I could see the prayers beneath. Fingers
that could wipe away my scars and
moles, polish me to ivory bone,
to deadly essence.

The only one in the house awake, the
only one in the whole of Scarborough, I
knew His holy face would never be calm,
never stop glowing, until I was good and
gone. Such naked love, wanting me
for all eternity. The picture frame, the
wall, the brick beyond, they all
dissolved, the stars grabbing at me
with greedy fingers.

Not until 17 did I replace that picture
with a poster of Jimi Hendrix
wrestling with a blinding white guitar.
Now Christ could only reach me
with childhood memories, a
giant octopus looming from
a picture book sea, a world
aeons beyond my Aztec curtains
and lava lamp. An occasional
nightmare: a severed hand
sharing the same white maggot pillow,
or a disembodied finger
lifting my lashes, the light
as bottomless as a tidal wave.

Octaves

Those Sunday morning marble clouds
didn't have a chance
once the bass and the soprano
hit the same helpless note.
They rolled away like thundering tombstones,
the sky as naked as veins
on a baby's wrists.
Not to mention chestnut leaves
shivering their ridges

or marigolds inhaling themselves
like smelling salts.
Telephone wires humming, distant cousins to piano strings.
Rickety gates knocking,
hinges made of the same impatience
as tambourines.
The weekly Chihuahua begging
to be a larger part of everything.
Right there in front of my eyes
a woman's teardrop earrings
swinging against her jawbone,
a blonde girl's ponytail
cracking up a bright crescendo,
an old man's bald spot
bouncing lasers off the walls.
How great thou art,
I sang along,
teeth whistling in chaotic harmony,
the hairs on the back of my neck
lifting me through octaves,
up the holy chimney
above the rolling clouds
where blue was the colour of God
listening,
holding his breath.

Barry Dempster
In the Beginning Was The Word

"In the beginning was the Word," begins John's account of the birth of Christianity, a story with which my gargantuan childhood ego avidly identified, having been listening to God for as long as I could remember. Sunday mornings in the Scarborough Brethren Gospel Hall were one long string of Bible verses, precarious syllables warning me about the dangers of doubt and worldliness, promising me the top prize of eternal life. In my beginning too, the Word was everything, the very source of consciousness. Being religious was an ultimate adventure, an inner life like William Wyler's big budget Ben Hur.

I don't remember seeking out much poetry as a young child beyond the usual nursery rhymes and riddles, but I knew all about the incredible energy of language. Early on, David's battle with Goliath and Daniel in the lion's den were practically boiling over with dread and anger. My Sunday school teacher used words like "wrath" and "ravenous" and the shiver going up and down my spine was both hot and cold at the same time. Sunday mornings made the rest of the week as dull and safe as living inside the lines of a colouring book. I ached for God's high stakes, His impossible rules. At the time, I figured being that close to the mystery of the universe made me a disciple and I dedicated my enthusiasm to dodging sins and somehow living up to it all.

Now in these clearer, less drastic days when my spirit has flown the Brethren coop, I realize how close I was to fundamentalist distortion, losing myself to judgment and fear, without the imagination to appreciate subtle words like "tolerance" and "grace." Still, without those crazy opposites of hellfire and salvation, without the constant warnings, the fiery tears and dizzying praises, I wouldn't be a poet. Poetry comes from extremes, from the left field of all experience, and my passion and impudence came straight from God.

American poet Mary Oliver writes, "In art as in spiritual life there is no neutral place." I came to poetry as a fanatic, my confidence shaken by discovering a distance between God and myself. Some of the words I was insistent on were all mine, while others, God's favourites, were stuck to the roof of my mouth; I could still remember what they'd felt like rolling down the length of my tongue. But this new adversarial God was every bit as personal as the former all-encompassing one: God the father, my father, God the first and final word. It took a lot of loneliness and anger and listening to the powerful Word(s) of others before I began to loosen my hold on that long-ago beginning. "Jesus Christ is the poem God made," Oscar Wilde said, someone the

Scarborough Brethren Gospel Hall would never ever quote. So, from personal God to poet God, the long, exhilarating journey from the literal to the metaphorical. I was awed by the inclusiveness of this new view. I stole pages from the Bible, mingling in a little karma, a little nothingness, adding a few lightning scribbles of my own. "In the beginning...." With each new word, a small enlightenment, another way of looking at heaven and earth.

As my faith stretched itself beyond that tiny suburban Gospel Hall, so did my poetic vocabulary. I began learning a string of wonderful new words like Rumi, Milton, Issa, Wordsworth, Rilke, Lawrence, Eliot, Neruda, my ears brimming over with the music of so much assumption and audacity. Kathleen Norris says it as simply as it comes, "Poetry, like prayer, is a dialogue with the sacred." I realize that I've known this ever since that first time I heard God talk.

Sky Dancer Louise B. Halfe

LOUISE BERNICE HALFE, also known as SKY DANCER, was born in Two Hill, Alberta. She was raised on the Saddle Lake Indian Reserve and attended the Blue Quills Residential School. Louise earned her Bachelor of Social Work from the University of Regina, and a certificate in Drug & Alcohol Counselling from the Nechi Institute. While attending the University of Saskatchewan, she wrote her first book of poetry, *Bear Bones & Feathers* (Coteau 1996), which was shortlisted for the Spirit of Saskatchewan Award, the First Book Award, the Gerald Lambert Award, and eventually won the Milton Acorn Award (1996). Some of her work has appeared in various anthologies and magazines, notably *NeWest Review.* Louise has been on the CBC's "Morningside" with Peter Gzowski, "The Arts Tonight" and "Ambience." She has been a workshop leader in Banff with Rachel Wyatt and Robert Kroetsch, and has travelled extensively across Canada doing readings and presentations, as well as abroad. Sky Dancer Louise's second book, *Blue Marrow,* a mixture of prose, poetry and journal writing, was published by McClelland & Stewart in 1998. She is married and has two children, one of which has made her a proud grandmother.

Ghost Dance

I shall not be there. I shall rise and pass. Bury my heart at Wounded Knee.

They are in hills,
in bush and prairies
clattering
shattered bones
chattering
laughing the dark.

Star after star
the wind carries the knuckle of
whistling songs.

They dance
gathering quills, moss
clay, feathers and
bear bones
to flesh themselves.

The drum beats
Big Foot
dancing
whistling eagles
laughing, laughing
these shattered,
gathered bones.

Spirits

The veins throb
splattering
red the sky.

Comes the
night travelling
blood
swirling skirts
lifting
swishing moccasins.

Swaying bodies
in the beat of rawhide
in the beat of drum
the breathing Native lung.

Nodding heads
join swinging hands
shuffling deer-skinned feet
sweet bodies

babies
released from
the belly tie
spurt blood

Cover hay and furred bed
wolf-mother rejoices,
echoes the chant.

Red sky, night travelling
sweet bodies, four-legged ones
wolf-mother's blood
wolf-mother's voice

Dancing, dancing the union
swirling skirts
moccasin feet.
The beating common lung.

*Pāhkahkos**

Flying Skeleton
I used to wonder where
You kept yourself.
I'd hear you rattle about
Scraping your bones

I opened a door
You grinned at me
Your hollow mouth
Stared through my heart
With empty eyes.

You lifted your boney hands
To greet me and I
Ran without a tongue.

You jumped on my back
Clinging to my neck you hugged
My mound of flesh.

For a thousand years you were
The heavy bones
The companion who would not leave.

You knocked your skull
On my head
I felt your bony feet.
I dragged and dragged

I couldn't carry
Your burden more.
I pried you loose
Bone after bone.

We stood, skull to face
Pāhkahkos, your many bones
Exposed
I, lighter than I could stand.

I fed you the drink of healing
Your ran skeleton fingers
Down your face and onto mine.

I gave you a prayer cloth
I wove a blanket of forgiveness
You covered us both, skeleton and flesh.

I gave you the smoke of truth
You lit your Pipe to life
You lifted it to your ghostly mouth,
To mine.

My *Pāhkahkos* companion,
My dancing Skeleton
My dancing friend.

We carry our bundles
Side by side
Bones and flesh.

**Pāhkahkos* = Flying Skeleton, mythical spirit of the Cree

Nōhkom ātayohkān *

Nōhkom ātayohkān
a crown of sage
covers long strands of
fringed brome hair.

Ravines cut through
the soft leather
of your face.

Your mouth a
sensuous pink
wintergreen,
the movement of your long
strong neck
a graceful tree.

Old one with laughing eyes
wrap me in blanket grass
fragrant with sweet pine,
the woman-musk
of your rainfed forest.
Ground my wandering feet.

I want to cup
your breast,
a starving suckling child.
I want to drink the black and
white prayer beads
your milk spills.

Nōhkom
there are no barren lands
only a searching *ayisīniw*
snared in you.

**Nōhkomātayohkān* = Grandmother of the legends; *Nōhkom* = my Grandmother; *ayisīniw* = human being, person

Elder's Waltz

Nōhkom and *Nimosōm*
are going dancing

Tobacco offerings
ribbon cloths
Elder's murmuring
prayer songs.

Nōhkom wears pony beads
flowing flowered dress
a wide beaded belt with
hanging silver trinkets.

Campfires
muskeg tea boiling
smoke
meat drying.

Nōhkom and *Nimosōm*
are going dancing.

Nōhkom has been working for hours
on her deer-skin moccasins
soaked in tea
kneaded and stretched
dried like flannel.
Nōhkom lifts leathered legs
tugs and pulls
wraps and wraps the
hightop flaps and
rawhide thongs.

Chokecherry leather
pemmican pouch
kinnikinnick green
briar Pipe.

Her long blonde-white braids
greased with bear fat
gloss as if she's spent
hours with her porcupine brush.

Nimosōm
cropped blonde-white hair
slicked down too with bear fat.
He slips on buckskin quilled jacket
over his velvet tanned leggings.
Beads and beads sparkle from
moccasin feet.

People laughing
skynight
sparking
with fire embers.

He searches for the white-skinned drum.
His footsteps shuffle dance
to music in his head.
Tonight, tonight
the departed spirits
will feast on the bone's marrow.

Nōhkom and *Nimosōm*
are going dancing.

People squat
hands touch
circle forming.

The white-skinned drum
sends its musical tongue
colouring the air.

Blueberry, sweetgrass
offering and burning.

Nōhkom and *Nimosōm*
are dancing.

**Nōhkom* and *Nimosōm* = My grandmother and my grandfather

Possession took me last night.
I slept with a bone.
The jaw bone of elk lined with pearly teeth.
I bathed her in sweet grass. Laid her under my pillow.
Winds swept through me. This path has chosen me,
this chosen walk, is a blizzard white out.

My Cree-ing alone in this heavy arm of snow.
I hang onto this bone
dressed in satin. Wade into redberry lakes.
I am married
to her garden of carrots and sweet corn heads.
I lay her skull, broken jaws,
face them to the East.

When *Nōhkom's** granddaughter slept
on top of graves
I thought she was crazy. All night I danced
above her head.
She dragged a string of skulls, heavy
in torrent rains. Cree-ing loud into my night.

I sleep with rocks too.
I couldn't say this before.
Who could I say it to 'Xcept *Nōhkom's* granddaughter?
The rocks fill me. Their stories,
slates in dreams, heavy in my stomach
move like thick clouds blown by my laboured breathing.
I cannot catch them.

I don't think to ask them
to slow down.

I sleep with petrified wood too.
Frozen snails, snakes with amber eyes,
crystallized tails.

Soon the black robes
will burn me
stake me to their cross.
I won't have to live
in whiteouts much longer.

**Nōhkom* = my Grandmother

*Pē-nihtacowēk, Nōhkomak**
Climb down, my Grandmothers.

Pē-nānāpacihinān
Come heal us.

The thick fog, the fog has lifted.
The ice shattered

Kwahkotēw, nipōnēnān
The fire burns, we have built the fire.

The crossing of the roads
is where we wait.

Pē-nihtacowēk, Nōhkomak
Climb down, my Grandmothers

Pē-nānāpacihinān
Come heal us

Ē-sōhkēpayik. Ki-maskihkēm.
Your energy so powerful.

Kā-wī-nanāpacihkoyahlc
We need for our healing

Pē-nihtacowēk, Nōhkomak
Climb down, my Grandmothers.

Kitimākinawinān. Sawiminān.
In your gentleness pity us.

*The English translation follows the Cree in each stanza.

Ram Woman, we met for the first time.
You stood on top of graves at Whiterabbit,
large eye staring.
My legs wrapped my husband.
Your head thumped those stones.

Ram Woman, I stood naked
beneath the falls.
Your hoofs pounded
in that April rain. I remember
your fist in your mother's womb,
heels kicking her door.
When her lips split
two birds flew
from your mouth. You
lifted your moccasins
in a Ghost Dance.
While the drummers sang
dogs ran after your meat
and bones, pissed at your feet.
You let them in. They left
nickels and dimes.

Ram Woman, always in pursuit
of the laughing sun,
the pregnant moon.
A gorging river, you plunge
heedless into the spring fire.
You drag your laughing weeping
child in a trail of snares, shutting
out the wind.
Ram Woman, Ram Woman,
in Kootenay Plains you sang,
lured me to your grave,
gave my heart a twist and
sent me flying, gave me
your large eye
for my stepping stone.

Sky Dancer Louise B. Halfe
The Tears that Wove Our Songs

She came in a Vision, flipped many faces. Stone-aged wrinkled, creased like a stretch drum, thin flesh, sharp nose. When the Sun sleeps she takes faded rays, dresses her gown. She's the burnt rose of autumn, a blue-winged warbler. The awakened river flanked in every woman, rolling pebbles over and over till stone eggs are left. I travel with her youth, this Night Mistress. Hair fresh, sweet grass braided in perfection. Long ago Grandmother danced in glades, women crushed chokecherries, saved the blood, cleaned porcupine quills, wove them into birch baskets, chewed sinew. They drummed, danced, lifted their dreams. Ribboned the Sky. Raw-boned, they left their blood. In these moccasin gardens I pick my medicines.

I talk to Magpies. Their eyes my Womanhood. How can I mark that? The first ecstasy of climax? Each squealing baby? When told to cross my legs at ceremony? When told never to walk over men when I was in Full Moon? Or was it the first time I gave away all my jeans, sexy dresses and wore tents for a year? Did our Grandmothers know we would be scarred by the fists and boots of men? Our songs taxed, silenced by tongues that speak damnation and burning? Did they know we would turn woman against woman?

Did they know some of us would follow, take mates of colour and how the boarding of our worlds would pulse breathing exiles connected to their womb? Did they know only some would dig roots, few hands calloused from tanning? Did they know only a few would know the preparation of moose nose, gopher, beaver tail feasts? Did they know our memory, our talk would walk on paper, legends told sparingly? Did they know of our struggling hearts?

Each month Grandmother waxes and wanes, pregnant with wolverine and baying dog. I become heat at Midnight, a yowled cat, fingers stained. Quills. Mark these songs.

We are Star people. *Wēsākēcāhk** sang to the Water people to bring back Earth from where we dove. She pinched the mud from the exhausted Muskrat. Blew Yotin. Blew *Iskotēw*. *Iskwēw* was born. *Pimātisiwin* fills woman. Man is born. I return to the Moon glade, turn up the sod, lift my songs. Dream. Grandmother dances at Midnight. Grandmother Moon, my Shadow dreams the dark.

Grandmother, the Woman in Me.

*Cree terms: *Wēsākēcāhk`* = Cree trickster; *Yotin* = Wind; *Iskotēw* = Fire; *Iskwēw*= Woman; *Pimātisiwin*= Life, Movement, Creation

Dennis Lee

DENNIS LEE was born in 1939 in Toronto, where he lives and writes full-time. He is married, with three children and a grandson. Co-founder of House of Anansi Press, he received the Governor General's Award for Poetry for *Civil Elegies and Other Poems* in 1972, and is the author of *Kingdom of Absence* (1967), *Civil Elegies* (1972), *The Gods* (1979) and *Riffs* (1993). He has edited *The New Canadian Poets, 1970-1985* (1985)and written the critical work *Savage Fields: An Essay in Literature and Cosmology* (1977). He is the author of *Alligator Pie, Jelly Belly,* and other books for children. His most recent adult collection is *Nightwatch: New and Selected Poems 1968-1996* (1996); *The Ice Cream Store* (1991)is his latest volume for children. He has recently published a book of essays, *Body Music* (1998).

The Gods

I

Who, now, can speak of gods—
their strokes and carnal voltage,
old ripples of presence   a space ago
archaic eddies of being?

Perhaps a saint could speak their names.
Or maybe some
noble claustrophobic spirit,
crazed by the flash and
vacuum of modernity,
could reach back, ripe for
gods and a hot lobotomy.
But being none of these, I sit
bemused by the sound of the word.
For a man no longer moves
through coiled ejaculations of meaning;
we live within
equations, models, paradigms
which deaden the world, and now in our
heads, though less in our inconsistent lives,
the tickle of cosmos is gone.
Though what would a god be *like?*
Would he know about DNA molecules? and
keep little haloes, for when they behaved?...
It is not from simple derision
that the imagination snickers;
but faced with an alien reality it
stammers, it races & churns for
want of a common syntax and,
lacking a possible language,
who now can speak of gods? for random example
a bear to our ancestors, and even to
grope in a pristine hunch back to that way of being on earth
is nearly beyond me.

II

And yet—
in the middle of one more day, in a clearing maybe sheer
godforce
calm on the lope of its pads
furred hot-breathing erect, at ease, catastrophic
harsh waves of stink, the
dense air clogged with its roaring and
ripples of power fork through us:
hair gone electric quick
pricklish glissando, the
skin mind skidding, balking is
HAIL
and it rears foursquare and we are jerked and owned and
forgive us and
brought to a welter, old
force & destroyer and
do not destroy us!
or if it seems good,
destroy us.

Thus, the god against us in clear air.
And there are gentle gods—
as plain as
light that
rises from lake-face,
melding with light
that steps like a skipping-stone spatter
down to
evoke it,
till blue embraces blue, and lake and sky
are miles of indigenous climax—
such grace in the shining air.

All gods, all gods and none of them
domesticated angels, chic of spat & wing,
on ten-day tours of earth. And if
to speak of "gods" recalls those antique
wind-up toys, forget the gods as well:

tremendum rather,
dimension of otherness, come clear
in each familiar thing—in
outcrop, harvest, hammer, beast and
caught in that web of otherness
we too endure & we
worship.
We lived among that force, a space ago.

Or,
whirling it reins into phase through us, good god it can
use us, power in palpable
dollops invading the roots of the
hair, the gap behind the neck,
power to snag, coax bully exalt into presence
clean gestures of meaning among the traffic of earth,
and until it lobs us aside, pale snot poor
rags we
also can channel the godforce.
Yet still not
abject: not
heaven & wistful hankering—I mean
the living power, inside
and, that sudden that
plumb!
We lived in such a space.

III

I do say gods.
But that was time ago, technology
happened and what has been withdrawn
I do not understand, the absent ones,
though many then too were bright & malevolent and
crushed things that mattered,
and where they have since been loitering I scarcely comprehend,
and least of all can I fathom, you powers I
seek and no doubt cheaply arouse and
who are you?
how I am to salute you, nor how contend with your being
for I do not aim to make prize-hungry words (and stay back!), I want
the world to be real and
it will not;
for to secular men there is not given the glory of tongues, yet it is
better to speak in silence than squeak in the gab of the age,
and if I cannot tell your terrifying
praise, now Hallmark gabble and chintz nor least of all
what time and dimensions your naked incursions
announced, you scurrilous powers yet
still I stand against this bitch of a shrunken time
in semi-faithfulness,
and whether you are godhead or zilch or daily ones like before
you strike our measure still and still you
endure as my murderous fate, though I
do not know you.

Nightwatch

Back with the scotch in the dark—how many
nights this way, old pal?
Lost in a judgment sweat, the rocky
tapes & jeremiads and around it goes again, *Y'gonna hafta*
serrve some-body; thankin
yew Mister Dylan.
But it's out past words, to the thrash of calamity midnight,
where the bass line skids like a whip, like
acetylene balm, like a liquid wisp of forever and
what am I being?
Lost in the dark, with a slam-bang case of extremis.
Lost in my molten body, a Molotov handful and from this instant I swear
I can change! I can change! tip it
over and momma keep smokin that bitch guitar.
Got a cache of christened bullets, one for each
pygmy self that lessens me, *crack!*—and
tonight, tonight I'm contagious, tonight I could
peel the lies out loud;
though where in my life is there blessing? and where in the world?

Old payoffs dissolve, in the crunch of letting go.
Codes of intent, whole plausible repertoires fold.
So. The dream of possessions expires, in a flatulent cackle—
and what did I think, that a man could be saved by commodities?
I swore it wasn't true but the lap-tops and tape-decks pour
through me, buy me off
easy, wave upon wave in the headlong race to thing heaven ...
(Slowhand riffs, like
feathers of pain in the dark.)
And payoffs at work dissolve:
twenty years of editing, and for
what? a few good books and people aside, to drudge in the sewers of ego,
of back-biting, back-scratching, spleen, and all to
speed the canonization of mediocrity as a national literature—
was that worth half my lifetime?
Let it go. It was one more lie.

And listen, I had this friend,
and for years I watched as he railed at our moral decay; we were
all on the make, or the take—I watched as the raging perfectionist
succumbed to a niggling success,
and the long, slow, lucrative slide to wised-up irony.
Sweet dreams in cynic hell, you curdled dreamer.
And applause of my scribbling peers dissolves, glad
hand of the also-rans;
I hankered for comrades but the tribe was founded on lies, and
dissolves the fellowship of failed ambition, bonhomie of
bile and abandoned ideals and how often I too went
whoring after approval,
forsaking the bedrock claim of the real for a mess of recognition,
the trophies of sellout.
Old shopworn camerados, who am I to judge you?

So, year by year and
numbed by success I went
wired to heavy mirages, a litter of
two-bit personae, till finally
shucked & plucked & dismantled I
hunker at last in my body,
and if there is even the ghost of a resonant *I* in the
blah-blah ego brigade I
cannot locate it, and lucid and pissed in a small room
how have I come to this?

And the dream-on salvation sorties dissolve, flukes of
auto-hypnosis and causes I leeched off, dissolve the inveterate
lies of a bankrupt marriage, dissolve my other vocation of
nurture for often I used the quicksilver empathy leadings to
get myself liked, a sensitive doormat, a moral eunuch and
dissolve and dissolve this knee-jerk curse and litany of dissolution—
I have collaborated in the falsification of my life
till spinny in gone light often I howl in myself, call down a
lethal wrath in the veins, move on, move on
oh mother mother was it for this you bore me?
And this I achieved in Canada, where I came by
generations of flesh and methodists to lucid dead-end,
though once I was whirled about and gorged on the

rumours of God I reached a voluptuous
make-believe, but better now to
drink the night to the dregs than drift in anaesthetic glory.

But I will say this.
It was
heart's largesse, to have lived a space on earth.
How precious the rain. And the pines. And the
night winds too, they were precious,
combing the houses' hair.
I have stood hushed to the quick: tethered by
rockface and boulder—mute jut of
molecular non-intent.
Or slash of raw sumach, scarlet past
scarlet in mind. And the merest
cloud changes, ten trillion per hour.
Everywhere, everywhere the harsh stark exquisite
tug of creature adherence;
I am no wilderness scout but there is a bodily homing which
I too was permitted to know.

But it's back to the shame and the
scotch, for as a citizen I
reneged. While my city slid to manhattan,
I stood by and clucked. And when the country, my beautiful
gutless Canada, lay back
and spread for a star-spangled buck,
in the time of the great betrayal, Mulroney ascendant,
I signed a crummy petition.
We cannot turn history back on itself but surely a
man can do more than watch, as the planet slides to ratshit.
Fat chance! for while we went
lurching towards apocalypse, old
mother adieu in the cradle and starfield of eons,
I wrote some cheques, and hoped it would all go away ...
Tippytoe! Tippytoe! I may not know what
human is, but I can say *No;*
I can say No to you, and you with your ostrich denials and
deeper, bury me deeper—I can say,

Creature world, extinct;
I can say, *Planet go nuclear come.*
And
deeper, wedge me down deeper, nobody has to see me;
pretty please, just a little bit deeper ...

When did it all go by?
The scotch is gone. My body's shot. And the years come
faster now, year by year they
come faster and
pass me with their cargo of bald spots and coronary alerts.
I have squandered whole decades, it's
late too late to start and yet too
soon to pack it in and one day, looking back
at the sum of my time on earth, bearing down
as the pain or the drug allows, half-claimed already
by the long goodbye and leakage of the grave,
what will I have that rings true?
"You're born; you jack off; you die—what
more, little window shopper?"

Sweet jesus, it's
hard. Hard to
sit and accept—there is nothing more to imagine,
right now is my life; and also, how
empty the night gets.
Night after night it gets
empty, for I keep
trying to heed the voice, and follow, and
yes—
but then there is nothing to hold,
and nobody holds me ...
How late I reached the place of no excuse.
How late I learned to ask, what does my
animal heart require?

But tonight,
in the lash and ebb and echo of the music,
the years and years a shambles, every
goal I chased a bad taste in my mouth—tonight
let it all go by, and carry me home.
Just let me
cease with honour once, where silver
birches tumble back to compost glory,
pain of the hunted recedes,
tall buildings tilt at last to their bed of
gravity, old men their
deaths and benedictions—all my
failures corkscrewing gently to rest, absolved,
absolved in the entropy pull,
as each creature is allowed its
downward momentum, and it is
seemly to lie in the place of oblivion.
Let me go home at last, and
if I do not rise again to the daily grind and betrayals,
all will be well, and the
night will be well, and every
journey into endings will be well.

Cadence

We know a place to be.
It is not the same
for all, yet for each there is
one subcutaneous claiming: the place we belong to,
where our humanness is home.   And it is more an
exquisite taunt than a dwelling, for mostly we scruff along
by scotching the hints and traces—and how should we
honour that place? It is hard enough to get by.
And there are places I love, but when I found the one that owned me
it was nothing I knew. For in my twenties, god help me I
blundered into a—
what? A luminous tumult. Where I went in my body's mind. Not knowing
what that place could be, yet sensing
swivel and carom and thud I called it
cadence, more flex than content and
us in it. Feeling the current
snake through my life like a leghold rumble of is.
Though all the words are wrong—the place was
not a "place," nor a "thing," and the going was not in my
"mind" and I didn't "go" there—still,
tumble and source and
vocation, and in that hush and quake of almost-words,
cadence is iffy but utter, preemptive, you
come or you go but you
do not possess it.   It is
given and gift, a daily grace of
what.   And
what I know of being claimed, and home, and thank you,
is drenched with that sojourn.

And it was there I spent myself, day after day, in my thirties, obscurely,
gone now, and it nearly took me apart
to weather the pang transitions,
for when I emerged half out of my tree I was
nowhere, I could not find good
distance with others—craving too hothouse a

union or blah from adrenalin crash and that
herky-jerky to-&-fro
abrades a marriage; I came unstuck; I got frantic I
went to live in career, for I could not honour the stillness
in worship or in words—
what claimed me, unfitted me. And then it deserted me.
Yet when I was present to presence
there was nowhere else to be, and when not
it felt like betrayal.
As tonight it does also.

Hunger

Looking back—what made me run? What pushed me
year by year by year
through all those loves and jobs and drafts and last-ditch causes?
It was hunger. Hunger. And, deeper than every
nerve-end purr in the pleasure machines of the *polis*, it was
unfilled hunger. Though for what, I can't tell.
Outside the museums, the names of the sacred no longer work.
They say too much, they say nothing at all and
though it seems strange to me,
I cannot find words to declare what my heart was hungering for.

For the old ones grew exotic.
Marduk, Loki, Vishnu—
amen of dispersal;
Manitou, Ishtar, Zeus—
rustle of silent goodbye.
They have become a rare, achieved, and
dangerous hole in the species, residual nothing,
the space a passing makes—
Yü-huang, Utnapishtim, Quetzalcoatl;
Persephone, Yahweh, God.

For we rose. And thought. And trashed our sacramental
birthright.
But I have lived 45 years, and never once
have I inched beyond the safety of lament ...
But that's not what I *feel.* It's a playful itch,
a volt of desire, which
hankers towards what
God was a blasphemy of—never yet
have I danced full-tilt with my secret appetite:
to live in awe.

To live, at last, in awe.
And I know, many reclaim that
sanity at the margins, where our bodies still sense
the tang of indigenous meaning. Returning to
granite, to cedar and loon—old
amniotic siblings.
Or, catgut hosannas; held in that burnished ache of sound, how the
soulmeat champs and respires!
Even graft and torture provoke it, the outraged
sense of a justice we half belong to, half can't find.

But now we live
closer to zero noon, and what I know best
is the simple need.
To flare in the wordless dimension. To hunch in my
other name, that doesn't have
I all over it. Almost it hurts to relax.
But in that arterial stammer, my back to words,
the yen just breathes.
No storms of presence. My mind still yacks and fidgets.
But hunger hungers, and
sometimes I am permitted to mooch in the nearness.

Heart Residence

That creatures are not enough.
Hawkmoth and tanager snag me; muskies re-
call me, though alien in weedkill; raccoons
with their savvy instinctual poise haul me back to earth and,
wired in their unwitting circuits, bobtail and carapace all
species invade me,
tangling my reified soul once more in the bone fraternity
of things that are born and die—
yet though I crave it,
kinship and diastole the
creatures are not enough.

And roots are not enough.   Such
bounty I came to! heart residence on earth, and I have loved
a patch of ground too well: confess, confess at
dusk each summer long how a boy stood
claimed by the hush of the Shield—the slow dark
blotting the pines, and across the fretted
lake the loons re-echoed, and the excellent chill of infinity
entered my blood to stay as I went on listening, went on
listening.   I was practising my life among
rocky companions, but the
place is gone.

People, I hear we are catastrophe.
I hear we are strangers here.   For though we
re-fashion earth in our image,
though in our hunger to nest we disnify the real,
I hear we have no home. No
home but hunger.

And precious, precious the dear ones—but also, that
dear ones are not enough. What man has been
lucky in love like me? raised in a warm, in a
principled sprawl of a family; gifted with luminous
friends, who make low-rent jokes and live their lives nobly;
and quickened by eros—hard in its seasons, but holy and
gracias, rare woman; and children who fasten my heart.
Yet what will endure in time? and whom do I own?
Was I not given such
peerless companions that I might learn to say, in love, *Not
you, dear heart; nor you; nor you—
go by?*

DENNIS LEE
EXCERPTS FROM "POETRY AND UNKNOWING"

You've been called a philosophical poet. Is that accurate?

Some of the time. But more basically, I'm a meditative poet.

When I was starting to write, back in the sixties, I was very caught up in analytic thought. But I hadn't sorted out the difference between that kind of thinking and the meditative process. So my first book was logjammed with discursive ideas, or at least allusions to them. The poems were "intellectual," maybe even "philosophical." But enacted meditations they weren't.

Part of the problem was technical. It boggles me now, but Kingdom of Absence was a sequence of sonnets—some of the pieces being structured as sonnets, others kind of bouncing off the form. Which was exactly the wrong way for me to be writing, in these tight little pre-set units. The lope and sprawl and opening out and looping back that are intrinsic to meditation had no room to breathe, to stretch out and go anywhere. It was so tight-assed. Eventually I discovered that writing a meditation involves—certainly the mind, but also the heart, the body, the spirit. It's a quest, a quest of attending, and it unfolds on all those wave-lengths. And that's what I had to learn to do on the page. [...]

"Cadence" is a key term in your poetics. And you've spoken of how hard it is to spell out what it means.

I still get tongue-tied. "Cadence" is my name for the flux, the felt and living flux that poems rise out of. It's where the voices come from—it is the voices, intuited first without words. And the experience is very direct, there's no theory involved. But when this polyphonic tumble is coming through, the sense I get is that I'm a function of it, rather than vice versa. Only how do you talk about that, when talking depends on it? [...]

You mentioned Simone Weil as a touchstone or influence. How important has she been to you?

I tried to read her for years, but I couldn't connect. Then something got through to me—probably *Gravity and Grace.* When I read her now, one minute I think I see what religious genius means, in a way I never did before; and then two pages later I'm thinking, this is wacko. All that numerology, or the bizarre notions of

...and then suddenly, wham! we're back into stuff that stops me dead in my tracks. So I'm agog but wary.

I'm tugged by people who belong to the contemplative tradition, in some version of the negative way. I locate Weil there, though in mid-twentieth-century terms. I guess the work that speaks to me most in the high tradition is *The Cloud of Unknowing.* But also Pseudo-Dionysus, Meister Eckhart, Tauler, Teresa of Avila, John of the Cross.

And then there are people in recent centuries who were intrinsically part of that tradition, though they didn't necessarily know all their forerunners. Hölderlin. Celan. Weil, as I said. Eliot in *Four Quartets.* Heidegger—Heidegger is so problematic. Believe me, this is not a list of the people I find most cuddly. Half the moderns are crazies or bastards ... Merton, who was neither of those. I'd also go to Beckett, Giacometti, Rothko, Webern. Hector de Saint-Denys-Garneau is one of the few Canadians I can identify. Nobody has made much sense of this lineage in its modern phase, as far as I know. And I don't have it all straight, I just catch the affinities.

Anyway, this is the tradition I'm part of. The negative contemplative way. Majoring in poetry.

There's a line in Riffs, *"If I deny the luminous presence—/something goes numb at the core." And that echoes throughout your work. The gods have vanished, or we have banished them. We live in a kind of limbo, with symbols and myths and hand-me-downs and make-dos. But that power of divinity or spirituality, whatever word you put on it, is gone; yet it's something we desperately need.*

You're right, that hunger is central...Which propels me out the yonder side of poetry, for a spell at least. For twenty-five years intuition has drawn me to cadence, with the impulse to mime it in words: to polyphony as a way of poetic knowing. But intuition also draws me to hunker down in the "oblivion of eternity," as Leo Strauss or somebody calls the condition of deprival you speak of. Both those vocations are second nature to me. But even though they're intimately connected, they're not identical. "Knowing" stands on its head when it comes to the hunkering down; it stops meaning anything I recognize. And if you settle into the deprival deeply enough, it can become a version of the negative contemplative path.

I'd like to get at what that feels like: what it is, to be summoned to a knowing outside of language altogether. But for now I doubt I can do much more than clear the ground, point to the space where unknowing arises. What the experience itself consists of, I'll barely broach—partly because I'm a beginner, partly because it is intrinsically so hard to talk about.

When Eckhart or John of the Cross described the negative way, though—weren't they talking about something concrete? A specific kind of contemplative experience?

Oh definitely. "The negative way" wasn't just a general metaphor for going through a bad spell. First off, it referred to the experience of detachment: of being weaned away from possessing things. And it happened in stages. John of the Cross spoke of the dark night of sense, where you gave up attachment to things of the world—money, belongings, bodily pleasure. And then the dark night of the soul, where you found religious consolations being stripped away. Because the sweetness of contemplation had really been feeding a kind of spiritual materialism. Getting detached from possessiveness at that level was a far more radical affair; prayer went dry, God went missing, the works.

I remember feeling uncannily at home when I stumbled upon this tradition. The paraphernalia of late medieval Christianity and the Counter-Reformation was about as alien as it could be. (I was born in the suburban United Church, so you can imagine.) But that experience of spiritual barrenness as sacramental, the claim of naughting, unknowing—there was an immediate yes. I was an outsider, but still I came to it like entering my own skin. First in my teens, which was much too early; then in my mid-forties.

The great traditional accounts are austere and breathtaking; it's wrong to paste ten-line summaries onto them, and I won't even try. But there's one element that brings you up short from the beginning. The classic negative way proceeded, not by a dazzling growth of spiritual insight and ecstasy—but by detachment from those things. It didn't matter if they happened to you, or never did. But it mattered that you would almost certainly take them for the goal, the object of the exercise. And that is what you had to relinquish, that attachment; till you were simply waiting on God in the darkness. Sometimes, in fact, till you were simply waiting in darkness, period.

Why did anyone choose to follow such a course? No one *chose* to. And neither—given that the whole landscape has changed past recognition since then—neither does anyone choose to now. It claims the people for whom it is the right way. Anyone else has a comparable challenge, to find and follow the path that's right for them.

For you, it sounds as if Catholic spirituality provided the framework for entering this path.

It wasn't as simple as that. The sense of recognition, when I discovered the negative contemplative way—that was clearly a religious impulse. But on the other hand, traditional religious belief was not a possibility for me. There were believers galore in the world, many of whom I respected immensely. But I couldn't join them. I realized that in my twenties, well before I had any notion of why. How did a person hold those things together, though—being naturally contemplative, and being a non-believer? And where did writing poetry fit in?

I got a bit of a leg up, when I started to appreciate why classic statements of belief had so little purchase on me. Grant and Heidegger set me to pondering the mindset I'd absorbed from university on; intellectually, it seemed, I had a textbook case of modernity. Even if I loathed it.

These matters are more widely understood now, but they were a revelation to me at the time. Let me sketch them in broad strokes. After about 1600, a new cosmology developed in the West. Together with a new model of rational coherence, of how the mind finds order in the world. It was the paradigm of "objective facts" and "subjective values"—with the sciences exploring patterns of order which configure the facts, and with the status of the values getting more and more shaky over time [...]

This account of the "oblivion of eternity" spoke to me deeply. And at the same time, albeit on a larger rhythm, I was recognizing something else. It is fitting to be a citizen of secular modernity, and simultaneously to feel a great hunger. It's right to live in a world we understand as non-sacramental, and at the same time to recognize, without trying to leave that world or step outside that mindset, that you're not at home in it ... Yes, you inhabit modernity. But as an alien. A Martian. A seeker.

Accepting that still doesn't mean you can take refuge in the olden verities. Nor in New Age mumbo-jumbo. Maybe not even in a wonderful foreign tradition like Zen; not, at least, if you mistrust your capacity for self-indulgent tourism as much as I do. For better or worse, I'm a Westerner.

But those things said: it is à propos to be a secular modern, and to feel a hunger that the secular-modern world doesn't satisfy. You don't even need a label for your hunger—some rational category to legitimize it. Such categories are part of what triggers the hunger. Just declaring yourself hungry in modernity, with no name for what you desire and no agenda beyond declaring it, is an act of dignity.

I should add that—surprise!—I do know such hunger, and take it as a life-discipline. And at the same time I recognize that there are exemplary people, a majority I'm sure, who find reports of a nameless "hunger" thoroughly alien. Their way is different; for them to try to work up a hankering they don't feel would be daft. So if I explore a certain experience of incompleteness, of deep-down craving, I'm not suggesting it's the only matrix for living your life. It's simply the one I know.

Now we change gears. When you're young, you can afford to go haring after ideas like mad. Why not? You're going to live forever. But when you hit middle age there's a deeper crunch. If there's anything you've wanted with a passion, anything crucial you feel receding before you've even tasted it, then merely stroking ideas about that thing feels like a mockery. You have to go for it first-hand. Or forget it. The clock is ticking in your body.

About seven years ago, I reached that point with the hunger. Forget Grant and Heidegger, screw the Buddha and Jesus: I was hungry, and I wanted real food. Specifically, I wanted two things. To simplify my life. And to find a devotional practice—or else to discover, by looking, that I couldn't find one. I didn't know what either of those things would mean, but they were the leadings I had.

I won't dwell here on the urge to simplify. But what was the hunger for spiritual practice? ... Well, when I can locate it, which is by no means all the time, the hunger is like a subsonic tug. It draws me to hush, to awe. I can feel it stirring at one remove, so to speak, when I'm outdoors in the Shield, or when I'm listening to music, or making love. I think many people know it in similar ways. In these cases, there's a wonderful sense of hunger satisfied—with it being recognized as hunger only a half-beat later, as the joy of the body is taking hold.

But more often the tug is direct and contemplative—the impulse to awe pulls me immediately to stillness; draws me, with no intermediary, to centre and adore. Adore what? I have no idea. The yen just breathes, the question is not germane. And simply to dwell in that hunger, not to tamp it down, deny it any longer—that's already a relief. In fact, in a way that's opaque to me, to dwell whole-heartedly in the hunger *is* somehow to "centre and adore." Indeed, to be partially fed. Not in any fashion I might have fantasized beforehand; there's no sense of spiritual nourishment entering my system from outside. And if the whole thing transpires with no words or insights attached—well, welcome to spiritual life in the secular world. It means I'm called to worship without belief. For no reason, except I have to. In darkness; in muteness; in desire. And without setting aside my non-belief. What is just as primal as this awe is my inability to conceive a rationally credible *Something* that inspires it. I'm still a modern, my mind's not shaped that way. And there's also the moral outrage: how can evil get off scot-free? how can innocent people suffer so horribly? ... But what I came to see was that those things don't invalidate the hunger. Rather, they set the conditions for what I can do about it. I may be unable to "pray to God." But I can sit still—in awe, and active desire; and I can stop trying to possess what leads me to do so. Even by trying to "know" it.

Here's something that speaks for this unnameable hunger, something that gave me the shock of recognition. It was written around 1370, in *The Cloud of Unknowing.* "It is not your will or desire that moves you, but something you are completely ignorant of, stirring you to will and desire you know not what. Please do not worry if you never know more than this..."

For people with other paths to follow, that may be largely a bunch of words. But if you realize, you know what the words point to; if you recognize that sense of obscure, almost pre-rational arousal, of being stirred and claimed at a level so intimate you hadn't consciously sensed it was there—and without being able to identify what's doing the claiming, or even to bring it into focus as something separate from yourself—then the words go right to the quick. You know this experience, though you never knew you did.

You can live in that hunger as home. It's roomy enough. What's harder is to recreate, without merely trafficking in ideas, the things that come with it. The realization that "I" will never stop feeling hungry, or trying to possess. That "I" is specious to begin with, though it won't go away. That there is a deeper hunger feast—and a durable yes and agony—to which access is real. [...]

How does that discipline connect with writing poetry?

Oh man, that's a doozer. Polyphony and dark knowing; beautiful doozers. I still haven't got this straight.

I know that writing poetry, and secular contemplation in the negative way—for me, they're intimates. Both work intuitively. Both start by moving into a space of darkness, silence, attending. Both are life disciplines. They don't own anything, they're claimed by small openings.

But they're so different, too. What is the relation between kinesthetic cadence—which I know in a meat-and-potatoes way as a poet, even if it's obscure knowing—what is the relation between cadence and the ground of unknowing, where in practice I'm so radically disoriented I can't even be sure that "ground of unknowing" refers to "anything" at all? Are they the same thing? Two separate realities? I don't know how they relate.

And I don't even know the right mesh between the two activities. Sometimes I can practise both, sometimes one or the other falls away. These days I write.

I'd better just acknowledge the question, and let it breathe.

TIM LILBURN

TIM LILBURN has published five books of poetry including *Tourist to Ecstasy* (Exile Editions, 1989), which was nominated for the Governor General's Award in 1989, and *Moosewood Sandhills* (McClelland & Stewart, 1994), which received the Canadian Author's Association Award in 1995. He also is the editor of the essay collection *Poetry and Knowing* (Quarry Press, 1995). Due to be released, in 1999, are the poetry collection *To the River* and a book of essays, *Living In the World As If It Were Home.* He teaches philosophy and literature at St. Peter's College, Muenster, Sask. Since 1993, he has been associated with the Sagehill Writing Experience. He lives in Saskatoon.

Hosanna To Wisdom, The Divine Anima

Eye glitter in the alleluliaed corn,
gasp of thigh in the marigold, clover-candled,
deer fly fahrenheited acres, cleavage in the pear tree,
pear flesh pendulous,
cream-fat with sun milk:
                                        Dear, doe-eyed
beneath the Castilian fan of leaves, stalk,
fey Erato, Dearest, the debutante ego
of You sheens still from the self-ignited pumpkins,
the mustard forge,
bees burning corridors in the air, twanging
the G-string of the sweet pea!
Matter's purdah breaker, my eyes somersault and wheel
rolling zero-ed on the pollen core.

Deeper, dearer,
I court You, tigress of the electron jungle,
atom's tropic armpit fragrance, muscle grip
of nucleus, love clench, You,
Woman-spirit, spirit in matter, breast plated
with cabbage leaf, stork-bellied, You, God's feminine,
stun and stun and stun,
and cheer me in the roistering ventricle castle,
and skedaddle my blood like a first date.

Theophany and Argument

Oh
Blessed be all dapper goats natty in Kentucky colonel string tie tufts,
growing party hats of horn in absolute bewilderment, who ricochet, look!
from barn walls. Blessed.
Blessed be the jubilate of jump.
Blessed. Blessed.
Blessed be the red, banker's eye of pigs,
and raccoons, at nights, in cities,
kissing their faces in the ripe gleam of three, four Italian
tomatoes.
Blessed be fire
and dirt smell and root wonder
and the nectar-witted, blabbermouthed nonsense of negro-lipped tulips
that can be heard with one ear.
Blessed, blessed.
Blessed be the lunge-hearted, epiphanous urge of trout
at night-break, to silver heavily from the pond's upward eye.
Blessed be the eye.
Blessed be the sacred act of all looking.
And blessed be cataracted stones, who do not look, never. Blessed be
the stones, sightless, inward, monasteried in pasture corner piles, elders,
ancient ones, celibate, blue, dreaming of good gold, who chant
one magical Om
mouth to mouth with my choirboy ovalled cells.
Blessed be being, big-bellied being, bird song jointed, grace-legged
being, goat leap pulsed, holy dancer, with its holy metabolism
of storm, holy dancer, jitterbugging on the erect vowel, the *I* of stem, spine,
seam,
the phallic vowel of its triumphant self-announcement.
Blessed. Blessed be being and its hieratic law of more, its muscling out
phlox's purple desire muscling out,
and blessed be the eye-meet, crammed into sight look
of squirrels connoisseuring threat.

Blessed be.   Blessed be.
                                        Blessed be the eureka and the hick hurrah
And, necessarily, the discrimination.
Not star or fisheye, or fire, but consubstantial
with each glittering instance
my agape imagination
is the intelligent tip of cosmopolitan light, the pan-flicker;
is the astonished point, light's sublimity,
                                                        burning in my head,
aquiver, an awe that leaps ear to ear,
the slow, interior, Mona Lisa smile the universe ends in.
With sammadied molecules, with personed light,
                                                          with the spirit spurted muscles
of heart pounding life that bolts, I am Siamese-unioned,
well, at mind,
consanguine, a complementary fiction.

Let King Entropy stroke suburban temples with fingertips of weary.
Let the best in business suits walk blank from horror's sermons
mink-eager to knock up emotion and husband it again as decision
until the body winces with a moral astigmatism
before S.O.S.'s cue-carded in the given. I hear the vow-psalm
of gravity intoned by fraternal stones in the motherhouse of mud,
beneath stopped feet at intersections and beneath streets of distraction,
and am te deumed real, hallowed in the hesed of my heft, loved
into hereness by the nuclear hug, bodied proud in the hilarious spin.

The Green Lobe of God's Brain, From St. John's Sideroad North to Lake Simcoe

"External Nature, too, is divine,
mind slumbering in externality."
G.W.F. Hegel, *Philosophy of Mind*

for L.M.

Everything "dead" trembles
north of the apple-breathed horses and the Dominican cows, rocking
—O sweet Jesus—
slain by sleep, in their choir of hide-polished hazels
at Strawbridge Farm.
The under-earth from Keswick to Pefferlaw lights up with root flame,
Bolts, miles long, white, of vegetable lightning.
Here is the see of heron, bishop, diocese, here, of his living bone,
Parishionered by the barns, window-plain and pious,
Doukhobor-women-fat and their daycare
of the blonde, shirt-tailed corn
In its tag-playing melees, and by the haremed, churchwarden,
Tory bulls, spoken to by clover-fogged dreams
at dust roll;
North, pasture turning biblically to salt,
Sloughs meatier and milky as an old dog's eye near the lake,
creeks, trees growing
Out of water, the last fence line shrugging,
then walking under the coppery wash, everything "dead" trembles.
Corn-rowed clouds by day and by night, clouds
grapey as the curls of a too sensuous god, ecclesial podunkdom here
of bonebird.

A black man, nightly, here at the Savannah Hotel, in a petroleum tux, sings
Lux above his trancey Georgia organ *O bring back that lovin' feelin'*
O O O that mm-mm feelin'
As deer salmon-arc through maple lots,
their bum-stutter white as the soft dashlights of necking teenagers on milk-
blue roads near Bradford,

While beered-up potatoe pickers, in the wave-kissed hotel itself, workbooting
a yahoo, liturgical shuffle, their golden, froth-pumpkined
heads making them like Giotto saints, rise—*O O O O*—
Baseball caps first, now, through the hotel ceiling of cobweb and pine.
That feeling which is of hookah dreams
of the concubined bulls which comb the pastured Friesians smooth,
and of the blue towns, hereabouts, and of the green whirring cloud
over mill ponds,
the land's clear mind gathered from the white deer
copulating—flash-dot-flash—a holy Morse among aspens,
the Quaker quiet towns, the perfect apophatic fields,
and consciousness, gold, in vast purple afternoons,
within apples, Ida Reds, fallen
in hair of Hackett's orchard grass.
The earth's mind in its ghostly sleep.

At wood middle, heron, half a woman, council of one,
Raises his head of smoke.
He is gyno-glyph of the hysterical earth, word like the ideogrammatic
body
Of the one horse kept by the rich salesman at Hilltop Farm.
He is peace word, longlegged cypher of the hidden
Female world, and scribbles himself shakily across air.
He mounts in splendour vested to his pulpit in the dead elm.

That feeling which is the feeling nothing
dies. Nothing. Stouffville-ward,
a farmer feels the wobbly, white tongue
of the to-be-born in the Hereford's leafy womb,
calf's tongue white because it is the blind edge of the unseen
world sucking tit-wild at his fingertips—*aah, aah,*
say the farmer's hands.
He thinks, calf lined up, hooves in the prayer position
of birth, his arm gone to the shoulder within the earth blue bag,
of his wife making coffee up above.
That lovin' feelin' gospels the black
psychogogue, the Savannah's singer, the hardly-ever bird's vicar,
one last time,
through the snoring hotel.

Nothing dies.
And engines restart on the love roads; and in the wild raspberry
near the Jewish health spa by the rickety lake, one absent-minded
Oldsmobile
waits for the Resurrection.
Nothing dies.
Even the man-screaming-out-of-his-skin look of Rocket Richard
mongoosing across the Maple Leaf blueline on February 26, 1957,
thought lost forever, the look, perhaps a wholly new being,
obliquely cross-referenced in St. Dionysius' Divine Names,
has not died, but lives, here,
lives still in the brain of the deer who stops among aspens
and looks.
And interiored in stone, here in this place, is a dark magisterium.
And the awe of the first, now dead, cosmonauts here re-assembles
in the small facial bones of the hen-seeing, in dawn
light, fox.

The black man sings *O Oho-oommm,* away from the sleeping hotel,
walking to his car
a small suitcase of groans.
And somewhere, deep behind his ear, a subdivision house cat
At a-ha leap lets out a soprano thrill
That shivers long in the damp air. *Silentium, silentium*
in the green cloud of God's brain.

In owl-dom, in Hegel's mental sleep,
streams bellied like dancers, sleep-charismed cows vanishing
in ground cloud, at the bend of the theotokal root,
and in the joy of the white spiders singing, potbellied,
in the beams of the Savannah Hotel, even
The young men fighting in front of the Bradford Arms, the one
Lifting his toe into the crotch of the other,
The one tilting his forehead with almost adoration
Into the collarbone V of the other
Are together, lovers of sorts, in their eerie hallucination
of a womanless night.

Chant for the Feast of St. Francis

I love the tree.
It is standing to speak in the fire of itself.
It is great choirs rising to sing
the tree's long quiet.
I love the grass for it is strong.
I love the stone. Its dark eye
leans against my breast-knuckle.
I love the stone, the stone's here-next-to-us;
the *seriousness* of it holding itself
                                        just where it is
floats the world.
I love the earth, to sleep luminous in her ear.
The dead are beautiful, they are horse-shy,
their manners shining like chandeliers on ocean liners.
When we sleep
they crane forward to touch us and read
to us from their book.
I love the nothing that blooms in the dark
brightly
and is our last food.
Breathe softly
through the groin. Touch the tree, show
your palm to the stone.   Kiss the stone.

from *Moosewood Sandhills*

In the Hills, Watching

Among the nerved grass, thrones,
dominions of grass, in chokecherry dewlapped hills,
hills buffalo-shouldered with shag of pulsed heat, meek hills,
sandhills of rose-hip and aster, in the philanthropic silence
fluxed by the grass, hounded, nervous with its own uncountability, grass
the frail piston of all,
in the hill heat, lying down in the nearness of deer.
All knowing darkens as it builds.
The grass is a mirror that clouds as the bright look goes in.
You stay in the night, you squat in the hills in the cave of night. Wait.
Above, luminous rubble, torn webs of radio signals.
Below, stone scrapers, neck bone of a deer, salt beds.
The world is ending.

Contemplation is Mourning

You lie down in the deer's bed.
It is bright with the undersides of grass revealed by her weight during the
length of her sleep. No one comes here; grass hums
because the body's touched it. Aspen leaves below you sour like horses
after a run. There are snowberries, fescue.
This is the edge of the known world and the beginning of philosophy.

Looking takes you so far on a leash of delight, then removes it and says
the price of admission to further is your name. Either the desert
                                                  and winter
of what the deer is in herself or a palace life disturbed by itches and sounds
felt through the gigantic walls. Choose.

Light comes through pale trees as mind sometimes kisses the body.
The hills are the bones of hills.

The deer cannot be known. She is the Atlantic, she is Egypt, she is
the night where her names go missing, to walk into her oddness is
                        to feel severed, sick, darkened, ashamed.
Her body is a border crossing, a wall and a perfume and past this
she is infinite. And it is terrible to enter this.

You lie down in the deer's bed, in the green martyrion, the place where
language buries itself, waiting place, weem.
You will wait. You will lean into the darkness of her absent
body. You will be shaved and narrowed by the barren strangeness of the
deer, the wastes of her oddness. Snow is coming. Light is cool,
nearly drinkable; from grass protrudes the hard, lost
smell of last year's melted snow.

Discipline of Secrecy

Lie on your belly now, stare, pour into the golden
eye of the grain and be counted.
Engorge its face with your peering's heavy light.
The wheat gives you its plush inattention and
is therefore trustworthy.
It grew near your unborn face.
Let your weight bleed from you and fan into the wheat.
The wheat's moving rest will heft your desire and shape it
to itself.
Tell the wheat everything.
You have done nothing wrong and are naked.

You planted it by hand—someone to talk to.
The marrow of wheat is patience.
In its palm, the grain holds its one fixed heart,
nothing denser, nothing further away.
Ground is cold, sky lowered into it.
If you acted suddenly, not
watching yourself, the wheat's gold shadow, its
hiddenness, idea of beauty, would enter you
and make its home there.
Antlered wheat; like eros
it travels between the unknowable darkness
of sky and the unknowable darkness of earth.
The world is wide.
The wheat is trustworthy, sky thinking into soil.
In evening, thin pale flames over the fields, you see
this through aspens, the grain's ejaculatory flutter
under the aurora borealis.

Going into the Cloud

You must not think the drowsy, luminous weight, multi-breasted crops,
            loyal-to-itself grass, long conversations round a wine cup, will
rise, athletic, sure of itself, hefting from earth, heroing against light's
whispering thrust, wooed by the love of the One, nor
say all leaps against the decay of radiance, the flow downward which is
the debauchery of light, all things
leaping
to beach in the fixed, golden place
of a pure and distant absolute thinking, first place.

Desire nothing you can imagine.
You must sit on the thin hill grass.
Look south, open on your lap the heavy
                        perfumed score of weeping.
Return to your place and begin again.
The path to take
is to find yourself forgotten.

Gazing at the Wall

The furnace has wavered out twice;
afternoon moon in ice fog sags against earth.
Horse-calm hills and a mortal glimmer in air.
Ahead, in grass, beyond crouched snow clouds hulking through,
cliff edge of the century
and a black flicker of things that flow over it and are gone.

A brightness cakes the objects of the world,
grime of earlier seeings
and all we know.
The true world lives in a hovel further back.
Darker than chokecherry in winter, smart, out past hills,
rotting, past lynx trails, sunk down.
Light from us fattens us and loves us when we look at where objects are.
Time to learn to be homesick.

The air could kill us.
You walk through violet, embedded flames of cold.
You must recant the glamour of clarity.
The world, the world, you'd like to live inside a tree.
You have looked too hard for deer back in blow-outs and frozen
juniper, grasping for their marks on paths to place your
instep over them, this shining, have wanted to be let in, laid out grain
and waited, you have loved this light too much.

Take the dog, go through poplar deeper into hills,
the eye must learn an etiquette and exhaustion
before the distance of things.
Not a monk, watch the scoring deepen
as wind works a grass tip back and
forth across snow. This isn't prayer.
What's left is giving up entirely.
Everything falls short of theophany. It is itself.

Restoration

I want to be the knowledge that is one sleep in the sunward shoulder muscle
of the two-year-old doe coming out of hills and down to Moon Lake.
I will get there by seeing.
The whole body and virtue will rise up and form the look.
Seeing is the extreme courtesy that comes when desire is broken.
Desire will be broken and will continue with a bright limp.
We will move toward high bush cranberry and the smell of water.
I will be attentive, an oblique crescent near her spine, touched
by the light of her liquids. We will be going to Moon Lake,
the diamond willows,
old oxbow lake, reeds round it, the true river a ruin of water
in dust further on, the red century ending.
I will see my way into that place and into that body.
This will come only after I've been sitting in the long grass
eating loaves of shadow pressed up through the ground.
I will have been dreaming there of one day opening milky eyes and finding
myself sick, inside her body, high up, near the spine, poor, relieved.
Sometimes it happens: you lose everything
and wake in the strange room of what you want.
Except I won't be awake but asleep and full of gnosis.
In my ears, gold pulse of her footsteps.
We will go down the hill and enter the shadows of frost-burnt roses
and the shade of the smell of water in which reeds and elms are rotting,
October sunlight the shore of a country a small boat is just now pulling
away from.
I will smell her, light of one locked room in the mansion.
I will be in the muscle, a painting on the cave wall of her flesh.
I crane into the deer.
I am in the bright-dark cloud of knowing her
and could walk for days.
She is at the top of the hill and starting down
in early evening.

AN INTERVIEW WITH TIM LILBURN
(NOVEMBER 1996-JANUARY 1997)

SM: In naming spirit, the sacred or the divine, there is always a danger of falling into dualistic ways of looking at the world or parcelling out reality. Names and metaphors for the divine can limit, but metaphors are one of the poet's primary resources. Can you speak briefly about what brought you to the apophatic tradition ("negative theology") originally, and how this element of "unknowing," approaching the divine through darkness, "unnaming" rather than naming, has evolved in your work?

TL: I think it's a good idea to steer away from ontology and clarity when speaking of the sacred. Kant was right: we just stumble around when we attempt metaphysics. So maybe we shouldn't speak about these things if the ambition of our speech is to nail down. But our own desire (which, after all, is one of the roots of ontology) is more intimate to us and we can talk a little about it.

I think there is something in things, never satisfactorily nameable, that woos us, that we want to live with, that we want to come alongside. It feels to me like home and it appears unreachable. It is registered in longing, appetite. What is it? Who knows? Simply the world; or the unutterable complexity of things, the tolerance implied by this complexity; or the divine in things; or the hint of the union of all which is paradise—who can say? Attempting to say—choosing one of these alternatives and defending it—seems the wrong response to meeting it. It exposes itself to desire more than reason and it inspires, I think, an erotic life rather than a big explanatory system. And in the erotic life, all images finally are subverted.

For me, eros is quite an important thing and I draw what I know of it mostly from Plato in the *Symposium* and the *Phaedrus* and from Christian writers (like the pseudo-Dionysius) who have used Plato. Desire doesn't attempt to define; it simply responds, with a burgeoning singleheartedness, to the lure. And so the erotic person staggers forward, not knowing what she or he does, but knowing that there is nothing else to be done.

Words are cast up in this erotic straining but they are a singing, not analysis; they are the words of praise, even if they don't sound like praise. Such words undermine one another: something is this, something is that. But, fundamentally, the real speech in praising is desire: you "beat with a naked intent upon the cloud of unknowing," as the author of *The Cloud of Unknowing* says.

I first read that book over twenty years ago and was entranced, but understood it hardly at all. I've been reading it off and on ever since—it and other books like it, pseudo-Dionysius' *The Divine Names* and Gregory of Nyssa's *The Life of Moses* and many others. Desire slenders the person it sweeps along. This is another thing I try to write about, this bending of self by erotic momentum into a crude sign of what can't be said.

SM: *Moosewood Sandhills*, and many of your earlier poems as well, take a kind of "desert fathers" approach to wilderness as a way of reentering the world. Can you comment on how the current environmental movement may be a way of redressing the Cartesian split of subject and object, and how wilderness is important in your work?

TL: Descartes, for reasons he found overwhelming, was attracted to indubitability and he thought that this was unachievable except through reason. He was tremendously impressed by the undermining of sense-based knowledge by the Copernican revolution; the senses, he concluded, deceived and he sought to dismantle or discredit that frail bridge we have to the world. The mind for him was quite unlike the world—they're absolutely different things—but the mind can grasp the world if it shears it of those properties the senses know and love—smells, textures, beautiful shapes—and comprehends it as mere extension in motion. He felt that this remodelling—this impoverishing—of both the individual and of things would restore the whole of being to its proper state, with us as "masters and possessors of nature."

I think the mind is much more like things than unlike, but it has forgotten how to enact this similarity. I think it does this best now by simply refusing to be anything other than its failure to be in the world and by feeling the ache of its loneliness for things. You bed down with the river, with tree bark, long grass; you have nothing. The desert fathers and mothers did this too; they sat down beside what they couldn't know or contain and leaned, with great courtesy, into it. But this is the texture of every sort of contemplative life: you are ravished and discover you have nothing to set against the beauty that upended you. So you settle yourself beside it and look for your chance. You are all hunger and contrivance.

Environmentalism—one way of looking at it, at least—is an attempt to mend the split between mind and things that the Cartesian project sanctioned. Contemplation, the old monks taught, comes to sorrow; desire, they said eventually comes there. This is the environmental stance that most interests me now.

As for the bush, well, I just like to go there as much as possible; I like to live in it as much as possible. So much more, for me, seems to happen there.

Daniel David Moses

DANIEL DAVID MOSES is a Delaware, born at Ohsweken on the Six Nations lands along the Grand River in southern Ontario. He holds an Honours B.A. in General Fine Arts from York University and an M.F.A. in Creative Writing from the University of British Columbia. He lives in Toronto where he writes full time and works with Native and cross cultural arts organizations. His professionally produced plays are *Coyote City* (a nominee for the 1991 Governor General's Award), *The Dreaming Beauty* (winner of the First Prize, One Act Category of the 1990 Theatre Canada National Playwrighting Competition; later translated into *Belle Fille de l'Aurore* by Saskatoon's La Troupe de Jour), *Big Buck City, Almighty Voice and His Wife* and *The Indian Medicine Shows* (Exile Editions) for which he won the 1996 James Buller Memorial Award for Excellence in Aboriginal Theatre. *Kyotopolis* was produced by The Graduate Centre for Drama of the University of Toronto and *City of Shadows* and *Brebeuf's Ghost* by the School of Dramatic Art of the University of Windsor. *The Indian Medicine Shows* was included in *The Globe and Mail's* "Top 10 of '96" of Canadian Theatre. He is also the author of *Delicate Bodies* (poems) and *The White Line* (poems) and co-editor, with Terry Goldie, of *An Anthology of Canadian Native Literature in English* (Oxford).

To Susan

In the cluttered world between
stratus and pondface the greyest
one was the heron. That bird through

binoculars would open you
out like a lily. But I
held shut till it lifted off. What cut

me loose I glimpsed on the unfolding
wing. A blue edge of thin
colour. I thought of the high

sky showing jet trails curled
in a great and gassy
fleur-de-lis. I knew its bulb

could only be that tall
narrow bird. Ultimate flowers
are rooted in delicate bodies.

Evensong After Rain

The farmland comes riding
up from the west with the budding on
maples and barns with their houses in very

crisp silhouette. Where the smoky
blue ranks of the stratus have opened, the sky
is in the pink and the wet that slicks

up everything is gleaming, filled
with it. Though dark's closing in, the tint
remains in the spots our headlights blanch

out on the pavement. Somehow tonight it
even inhabits the movement. The furrowed and
fallow and winter wheat fields are sliding

along past either side of this highway
toward home and it feels like they're going
somewhere. Only our car and the evening

star are hanging in place. The dripping
world passes into dark while the rose coloured
light is curving through space.

Post Memoriam

Under her stone my Grandmother's
bones have got free. The years
opened up the last
hold we had, broke

the silk and dark wood from
around her. Now in the soil
she's becoming slowly
like water, growing cool

and clear as an under
ground river. Only
her bones and her gold
wedding band remain.

The gold wedding
band has turned off
of her finger and her bones
like the moon's

full light in
a night of stratus
are scattered and can
only wane away. But

the wedding band keeps
on turning down
through the layered
sediments, past

the lakes and seeping
streams. The bedrock is what
it seeks, is where at the last
its gold will open.

A Spider Song

I wait for black ferns and pines
to fill up with light after rain

and almost all my breath is gone
spinning across the cold. Oh on

the lake that breath joins up with mist
and grows so delicate and long

the moon turns round on legs and cuts
all uttering from the tongue.

The Corn

I'd already lost my hair. Now my sun-
fed children have been taken somewhere. Next

I'll lose these comfortable shoes of mud
to the cold, will be unconcerned. I no

longer need a firm foothold after all.
There's no flood of light anymore—to stand

in, to turn towards. The low sun's a trickle
that lays only shadows out (and they don't

move or fulfill one or feed some). Nor do
they do a thing for one's colour. One's left

with just these growing crystals of frost. No
childish ears to get brightly wet behind,

no hands to hold as you stand whispering
about the land. No one you could even

wave hello or goodbye. My hands caressed
the emptiness, grew as heavy as ice.

They dropped off; and, soon I'd guess the rest
of me will be ready to follow. Down through

the ice-bound soil to underground fields where
stars are planted in hills. At least that's what

I've seen, staring through the frost. Light will not
be lost but will grow and bud green again.

The Persistence of Songs

The people feed from the river and conceive songs.
But the strangers with the dead heads march towards the long
edges of their own blades. They see a thundering
fog along the horned horizon and turn around
to stalk the rising sun. They find four lanterns made
of skin arrayed along the river, the people
still feasting within. The strangers feed off their own
anger, flooding the river with blood. The four songs,
who are the children, go dumb and their white dogs mad
before the people have the strangers rounded up.

They bind them with skin from the fog and throw them in;
then, they wait for the river to heal. They try
to feast again. They pray to the children. By noon
the river grows an old skin and the children fade.
In the cold mud the strangers congeal. A fog
bleeds from the river, drowns the lanterns and stops up
the ears of the people with a dull, three-note song.
The strangers are praising honed edges and the white
meat of their own bodies. They curse the sun and vow
the moon turns so perfectly round they will square it.

They lurch up through the river's dull skin and begin
the marching again. The people search in the skin
for reflected light, the sunset or a lantern,
then assume the skin as mourning. The procession
the people enter tracks the moon through fog, cuts it
into quarters. And black dogs track the procession.
They feed off their own hunger and conceive a song
in praise of a perfect horizon made of meat.
That song fades; but, the four songs, who are the children,
return with horned heads. They feed from ears and edges.

Grandmother of the Glacier

The icefield she had in her head started
sliding the instant she died. *Was murdered*
would be more precise—would also explain
how her corpse became this high and open

ravine. But who's got the wit to split words
when that ice is coming at us? The world
can't ever again be that room we sat
in a circle in—the mainland rain hard

on a window as we listened to her
trying to explain about words. *Winter,*
she *grinned. That's the constant thought behind all*
our words. In Canada we never can

forget the edge on the wind. But the edge
on a knife cut in, cutting off more than
her words. So now it's hard to remember
how that edge and this cold thought grinding down

out of her head ever seemed separate.
Now they're a mouth that bites off and chews and
it's getting so close that breath flakes like snow.
So we go mute too—that mouth edge so red

that words drop from our own lips like stones. None
is as finished as those of hers that fell
into our hands. But the stars now are shards
of ice—they too are cutting in. There's no

time for her method—to split and polish
words against our own skin. Is that how hers
got so coarse she could embrace and contain
not only the stars but the rest of this freeze?

Her body's been swallowed. Ours may be next.
But even though we throw them in, her words
keep surfacing. May ours too be heard from
again—edging some terminal moraine.

A Shaman Song Predicting Winter

T*he sun is running down,* so the White
Bear says, *circling and wearing the track*
it cut into the sky right through. Soon

it will roll into the ocean. Though
it can't drown, that'll sure cool it off.
If you kayak out far enough and

look in, you'll see it looking up through
the night black waves, looking right at you
jealously, shivering like the moon.

A Story from the Mouths on a Beach

In the season of floes in the midst of
the pack a single great fish appeared and
along with some dozens of bodies of
ice came into these shallows on the flux
of the flood and bobbing here in the wash
of the ebb was stranded and exposed to

the air. Now it sang a song as these fish
usually do about the hues of
oceans and skies—though the version this sang
sinking into itself sounded as poor
as the hiss of a wave as it dies. Still
that got the attention of a babble

of children and drew them down from the cliffs
into a discussion of the fish's
skin and the stars they thought were beginning
inside. *Soon this fish will be up so high—*
a new constellation, sighed one of them.
We ought to try for immortality,

came the suggestion and the rest agreed.
Now in their concentration, incising
their names into the fish's skin, not one
of them caught the last note escaping from
its flesh, ringing like one of those bubbles
that breaks through the surface of these shallows

on the calm evenings in the season
of flies. Had they heard, would any have been
interested? Only the unearthly
attracts them. Now the children hurried off
toward some other song—it sounded as rich
as a cough—and so they could not witness

the way the skin of the fish went cold,
the way it iced over like the nameless
upper parts of this river must the first
nights of the season of wind. None of them
saw the final closing, each eye sinking
into decomposing flesh, each a half-

accomplished wink, a denial of both
twinkling and watery horizons. Now
only we who amplify and echo
the flood and ebb of your blood, who were washed
free of our tongues by the air and exposed,
can testify that the single great fish

did not completely die. Inside the few
remaining parts of it the song about
the hues of oceans and skies is still ringing
sweetly. And friends, those ice-coloured parts
will sing the song out again—though not till
the end of the final season of whites.

A Bone in the Balance of Moonlight

The moon, that heavy weight, pulled you out.
You'll never underestimate her
again. Had you ever thought her light

might lead you far into the dark or
hold you there so long the neighbourhood
park would empty? Why no one even

walks a dog! So maybe the moon's walking
you—has got you out of doors to do
your business. But what sort could you do

and with who when we're talking so poor
this gleam of pennies on the pavement
can also distract you? But the moon

knows who you are and where you belong
in the exchange of heavy and bright,
knows who among her daughters and sons,

the many and few, might benefit
from prowling the town with her, up for
all comers, after midnight. And boy,

she's done more than a few blocks and talked
you through to clarity before. Don't
blame her if you won't see what she's thrown

as more than bones. Her conversation
from now on concerns the currency
of blood, must be just with her daughters.

She'll give you no quarter, won't let you
go back to your room alone or with her.
You're here to spend those moons off the ends

of your fingers, to break the shining
line that pulled you out off in a spill
of silver. *Find the friend, the stranger,*

she says, *find the eyes weighty as coins*
with tears, with sweat, and soon you'll get to
put a new down payment on the night.

An Interview With Daniel David Moses (December 1996)

SM: How do you express or define "spirit"? What language, if any, do you feel comfortable using to talk about this region of experience?

DDM: I express it. Usually under the influence of red wine in the circle of my friends and fellow artists. On occasion, in the context of rehearsal or, best of all, in performance in the presence of the audience.

Somehow we stop worrying about the costs of living and working. Somehow we start dreaming up exciting stories or ideas or images. Despite the alcohol or nicotine or caffeine or natural disorder of our various metabolisms, or perhaps because of them, our various aesthetic techniques fine-tune the strings and skins of the stories or ideas or images to their tautest emotion. Thus clarified, that clichéd "heart" of the story or idea or image beats its moral power which is what it "means" to our lives. That, practically speaking, is its "spirit"—and more than—It's alive!—I don't need to say, being a practising, not a conceptual, artist.

(All this use of quotation marks to handle the word "spiritual"! Am I a child of the age!)

SM: You have suggested that whatever spiritual matters arise in your work come from an unconscious source, and that making them too conscious makes the work illustrative or academic. Could you comment briefly on your sense of the unconscious in your poetry?

DDM: I am well past the adolescent's so physical poetry, that welling up of words. Now my sense of my poetry is that it is unconscious, maybe even the unconscious.

If I'm lucky, some numinous and musical phrase comes to live and insist in my mind or on a page and I find myself following its direction into the language. And of course since I always think I know what I'm doing, I usually try to take the lead, hope to save time, and end ahead of myself, at odds with the poem, in a dead end, lost. I retrace my steps, check the original direction. Yes, this process is all fits and starts, best when I become somnambulant, at least for the first draft, the body muttering its dreams. My know-it-all-ness does become useful later on. It feels like the poetry is like that stone (I think it was) Michelangelo worked, trying to free the human form.

SM: You were brought up within an Anglican mission church on your reserve and you said you suspect your attitudes are a mix of that Christianity and traditional Iroquoian cultural norms. Can you comment briefly on how that mix plays itself out in your poetry?

DDM: Whatever appears postmodern in my poetry (if anything does) must derive from that mix of Christianity and traditional Iroquoian cultural norms that formed the place of my upbringing. My love of public language, ceremony, musicality, polyvocality and rhetoric, and my masculine feminism ("matriarchalism"?) were not addressed, were recognised only with puzzlement during my schooling. I suspect it now of being conventionally modernist, yes, that academic.

SM: Please talk a little about what you have called your "obsession with the moon." Does your interest in the feminine tie in some way to contemporary, practical spiritual revisionism in the native community?

DDM: From Iroquoia (see "matriarchy") come reports that the moon still looks as bright as ever, despite all the workings of the servants of the sun of god. I guess, from rumours that reach those of us working in the city, that "revisionism" is what's going down along the borders the indigenous world has with the immigrant one.

My own lunacy had to do with being masculine in a feminine world (see "Iroquoia") and, since moving to the city, has to do with being two-spirited in a materialistic world. I'm glad the moon's so bright.

Perspective is still interesting, despite what the voice-of-god narration might suggest.

P. K. Page

A writer and painter, P.K. PAGE was born in England during World War I. At war's end, aged two, she arrived in Canada with her returning parents. Raised in Calgary and Winnipeg, she was a member of the *Preview* group in Montreal and worked as a script writer at the National Film Board. She married Arthur Irwin in 1950 and lived in Australia, Brazil and Mexico. As a painter, she has exhibited in Mexico City and various galleries in Canada, and is represented in the permanent collections of the National Gallery of Canada, the Art Gallery of Ontario and many others. Her latest books are *The Hidden Room: Collected Poems* (2 Vols., The Porcupine's Quill, 1997) and *Hologram: A Book of Glosas* (Brick Books, 1994). Previous works include *The Glass Air—Poems Selected and New* (Oxford University Press, 1991); *Unless the Eye Catch Fire; Brazilian Journal* and three books for children: *The Travelling Musicians, A Flask of Sea Water* and *The Goat that Flew.* She has received the Oscar Blumenthal Award, the Governor General's Award for Poetry, the Canadian Author's Association Award for Poetry, the Hubert Evans Prize for non-fiction and the Banff Centre School of Fine Arts National Award. She was the subject of the film, "Still Waters" by the National Film Board of Canada, of a two-part sound feature, "The White Glass" for CBC Radio's "Ideas," and of a special issue of *The Malahat Review.* She has five honorary degrees and is an Officer of the Order of Canada.

Stories of Snow

Those in the vegetable rain retain
an area behind their sprouting eyes
held soft and rounded with the dream of snow
precious and reminiscent as those globes—
souvenir of some never-nether land—
which hold their snow-storms circular, complete,
high in a tall and teakwood cabinet.

In countries where the leaves are large as hands
where flowers protrude their fleshy chins
and call their colours,
an imaginary snow-storm sometimes falls
among the lilies.
And in the early morning one will waken
to think the glowing linen of his pillow
a northern drift, will find himself mistaken
and lie back weeping.
And there the story shifts from head to head,
of how in Holland, from their feather beds
hunters arise and part the flakes and go
forth to the frozen lakes in search of swans—
the snow-light falling white along their guns,
their breath in plumes.
While tethered in the wind like sleeping gulls
ice-boats wait the raising of their wings
to skim the electric ice at such a speed
they leap jet strips of naked water,
and how these flying, sailing hunters feel
air in their mouths as terrible as ether.
And on the story runs that even drinks
in that white landscape dare to be no colour;
how flasked and water clear, the liquor slips
silver against the hunters' moving hips.
And of the swan in death these dreamers tell
of its last flight and how it falls, a plummet,
pierced by the freezing bullet

and how three feathers, loosened by the shot,
descend like snow upon it.
While hunters plunge their fingers in its down
deep as a drift, and dive their hands
up to the neck of the wrist
in that warm metamorphosis of snow
as gentle as the sort that woodsmen know
who, lost in the white circle, fall at last
and dream their way to death.

And stories of this kind are often told
in countries where great flowers bar the roads
with reds and blues which seal the route to snow—
as if, in telling, raconteurs unlock
the colour with its complement and go
through to the area behind the eyes
where silent, unrefractive whiteness lies.

Three Gold Fish

I feel quite sure those three gold fish I saw
burning like Blake's *Tyger* in the pool
were real all right.
The pool was different too.
It seemed to swell
like some great crystalline and prismed tear
and brim and never spill
and those fish burned within it
burned and shone
and left their brand—
a piscine fleur-de-lys—
stamped on the air, on me,
on skin and hair
spinning to giddy heaven.

Sharp and clear
that fiery image burns within me still:
those three gold fish
the pool
the altered air
and I—observing and observed—
a high
point on a twirling spindle which
spun and hurled great gilded lariats.

The Filled Pen

Eager to draw again,
find space in that small room
for my drawing-board and inks
and the huge revolving world
the delicate nib releases.

I have only to fill my pen
and the shifting gears begin:
fly-wheel and cog-wheel start
their small-toothed interlock

and whatever machinery draws
is drawing through my fingers
and the shapes that I have drawn
gaze up into my eyes.
We stare each other down.

Light of late afternoon—
white wine across my paper—
the subject I would draw.
Light of the stars and sun.

Light of the swan-white moon.
The blazing light of trees.
And the rarely glimpsed bright face
behind the apparency of things.

For Mstislav Rostropovich with Love

Listening ear
a conduit for these sounds,
I watch your bowing arm
and see beneath
your sleeve, shirtcuff
and pliant sheath of skin,
a wrist of stainless steel
precision-turned,
fluid with bearings,
bright as adamant
with power to blind us
like a silver sun;
while gazing fearless
fire into fire
the enduring pupil
of my inner eye
made in the manner
that you made your wrist—
of matter primal and alchemical
impervious to accident
or hurt.

This is already much.
But there is more:
what falls apart is held together
each
atom aligned
and in its proper place.
So great an order interlocks my flesh
that I, as centred
as a spinning top
am perfectly asleep
(which, in this sense
means, if not perfectly
then more awake).

And as an atom—
one among these rapt
like-centred listeners—
I am part
of that essential
intricate design
which forms a larger unit—
mutable
around its sleeping core—
while it, in turn,
part of a vaster
one I barely glimpse—
already cosmic—
leads us to the stars.

Maestro, salud.
Perfection in an art
can heal an open wound
a broken heart
or fuse fragmented man.

Tonight, are we not proof?

Chinese Boxes

Box within box.
I know the order, know
large to small diminishing until
that cube the size of sugar—like a die—
is cast within its core
and therein set—dimensionless—
an all-ways turning eye—
a dot, an aleph, which
with one swift glance
sees heaven and hell united
as a globe
in whose harmonious spinning
day and night
and birth and death are conjured into one,
where seasons lie like compass points
and where, twinned with its answer,
question is born null.

Box within box.
From small to large increasing—
angles, blocks,
enormous, made of plexiglass,
the sky
filling with them,
visible as air
is visible when briefly smoked with breath
until their structures grow too large and sheer
for sight to encompass—
cellophane box kites
huge as the Kaaba
luminous as ice
and imperceptible to any sense
more coarse than sightings of that inner eye
which sees the absolute
in emptiness.

About Death

And at the moment of death
what is correct procedure?

Cut the umbilical, they said.

And with the umbilical cut
how then prepare the body?

Wash it in sacred water.
Dress it in silk for the wedding.

At Sea

True devotion is for itself: not
to desire heaven nor to fear hell.

Rabia al-Adawiyya, 8th c.

Rounding the salt-rimed deck
riding the tilting sea
sky grey
seabirds wheeling,
head down in despair,
in treadmill trapped,
in thoughts
revolving, churning, churning;
a stranger from a chair,
(one I had passed before
how many times unseeing?)
rose—and as if her words
were butterfly or bird
lighting upon my wrist,

blue butterfly of Brazil,
hoopoe perhaps or rare
landbird from who-knows-where,
weightless upon my wrist,
trembling brilliant there—
stopped the machine and brought
its grinding to a halt

and in that silence spoke

I don't know what she said
only that my despair
vanished and standing there
sky grey
seabirds wheeling
I knew as I looked at her
tweed coat and blowing hair
that she was Rabia.

Hologram

All that morning we looked at the citadel from every angle.
We began from the side in the shadow, where the sea,
Green without brilliance,—breast of a slain peacock
Received us like time that has no break in it.

The King of Asine George Seferis

It was astonishing, larger by far than we could imagine,
larger than sight itself but still we strained to see it.
It was Kafka's castle in a dream of wonder,
nightmare transmuted, black become golden,
buttresses disappearing in the cloud and azure:
a new geometry of interlocking octangles
and we, watching it, interlocked in a strange dimension—

that neither your heart nor mine could have invented—
of multiple images, complex as angels.
All that morning we looked at the citadel from every angle.

But that was later, after we had made the passage
from the faint light of morning star and pale moon
to unscrupulous noonday with its major chords—
battalions marching across an Escher landscape.
For us, at first, there was no hint of clarity,
no hint of anything that wasn't misty—
synaesthetic layers and lengths of space-time
leading us inward, downward, upward, as—
from all directions at once—observing closely,
we began from the side in the shadow and the sea.

Brave of us to begin in darkness. Or was it wisdom
that made us so prepare ourselves for that radiance
little by little? A Jurassic age must pass before even colour
could enter the scene—dawn's greys being so infinite
and infinitely subtle—tranparencies, opacities.
And then we sensed it together—the tremulous foreshock
of what lay ahead: what could not be imagined,
possibly not even dreamed, a new range of experience.
And—unbelievably—what revealed itself as earthquake
was green, without brilliance, breast of a slain peacock.

But to the cones of our eyes that green was shining
and pierced us like a spear. (When joy is great enough
how distinguish it from pain?) And after the fugal greys
and the near-invisible shafts of no-colour that had stained us,
how could our eyes adjust to so full a spectrum?
And yet in a flash, from infra-red to ultraviolet,
we saw the hologram glittering above us
glistening in air we could suddenly enter like swallows
as the whole citadel, rainbowed, immediate,
received us like time that has no break in it.

Presences

There they were as our guests, accepted and accepting.
So we moved, and they, in a formal pattern,
Along the empty alley, into the box circle,
To look down into the drained pool.

Burnt Norton T.S. Eliot

Extraordinary presences, the sunlight seeming
to light them from within, tall alabaster
amphoras with flames inside them
motionless within the grove, their shadows
like chlorophyl, like leaves, like water
slipping from a silver jug, reflecting
grasses, the long pliant stalks of willows.
And when they turned to us, their brightness spilled
over our skin and hair and, like a blessing,
there they were as our guests, accepted and accepting.

Only our golden selves went forth to greet them
that part of us which receiving blows
feels neither pain nor grief, the part that senses
joy in a higher register and moves
through a country of continuous light
shed by the one god, by the sun god, Aten—
moves as Nefertiti and her daughters
moved through their city of continuous light
in the pharaonic kingdom of Aknaten.
So we moved, and they, in a formal pattern.

Our feet barely touched the earth, and memory
erased at birth, but gradually reassembling
coalesced and formed a whole, as single birds
gathering for migration form a flock.
And some new incandescence in our heads
led us from the shadows to the sparkle

of Aten-light where we at last remembered
the arc of our lives, the distant stars we came from
and walked—O joy, O very miracle!—
along the empty alley, into the box circle.

And so to the maze with its forking paths which seen
from above, entire, was like a map—
or like a rose unfolding, a yellow rose,
opening in the unreflecting air—
the green of its leaves
the Garden before the fall,
every atom accurately aligned,
and there we walked in youthful innocence
until we came at last—new-born, royal—
to look down into the drained pool.

Planet Earth

It has to be spread out, the skin of this planet,
has to be ironed, the sea in its whiteness;
and the hands keep on moving,
smoothing the holy surfaces.

In Praise of Ironing Pablo Neruda

It has to be loved the way a laundress loves her linens,
the way she moves her hands caressing the fine muslins
knowing their warp and woof,
like a lover coaxing, or a mother praising.
It has to be loved as if it were embroidered
with flowers and birds and two joined hearts upon it.
It has to be stretched and stroked.
It has to be celebrated.
O this great beloved world and all the creatures in it.
It has to be spread out, the skin of this planet.

The trees must be washed, and the grasses and mosses.
They have to be polished as if made of green brass.
The rivers and little streams with their hidden cresses
and pale-coloured pebbles
and their fool's gold
must be washed and starched or shined into brightness,
the sheets of lake water
smoothed with the hand
and the foam of the oceans pressed into neatness.
It has to be ironed, the sea in its whiteness

and pleated and goffered, the flower-blue sea
the protean, wine-dark, grey, green, sea
with its metres of satin and bolts of brocade.
And sky—such an O! overhead—night and day
must be burnished and rubbed
by hands that are loving
so the blue blazons forth
and the stars keep on shining
within and above
and the hands keep on moving.

It has to be made bright, the skin of this planet
till it shines in the sun like gold leaf.
Archangels then will attend to its metals
and polish the rods of its rain.
Seraphim will stop singing hosannas
to shower it with blessings and blisses and praises
and, newly in love,
we must draw it and paint it
our pencils and brushes and loving caresses
smoothing the holy surfaces.

P.K. Page
From "Questions and Images" (1969) *

The last ten years span three distinct places—and phases—in my life: Brazil, Mexico, Canada, in that order. All countries of the new world.

Brazil pelted me with images. Marmosets in the flowering jungle; bands of multi-coloured birds moving among the branches of the kapok tree outside the bedroom verandah; orchids in the kapok tree, cucumbers in the kapok tree, the whole tree bursting into cotton candy. Flamboyantes in flaming flower against the sky as one lay on one's back in the swimming pool. Doric palms waving green plumage, growing antlers and beads. Cerise dragon flies. Butterflies as large as a flying hand and blue, bright blue.

Drums from the favelas beat like one's own blood; accompanied by the deep bass viol of frogs in the lotus pond; volleys of rockets shattered the black night air, air wet as a sheet and rank with the smell of decaying jackos. Insistent, less obtrusive, the tiny fret of tropical vegetation, the sibilance of bamboos.

Churches, golden as the eye of God, were so miraculously proportioned that one wondered if proportion alone might actually alter consciousness. Enormous quantities of gold leaf. Entire interiors of it, changing space, vibrating strangely; at one moment flashing to blind you, at another reverberating on and on like a golden gong. Moorish designs in tiles and lattices created infinities of intricate repetition.

My first foreign language—to live in, that is—and the personality changes that accompany it. One is a toy at first, a doll. Then a child. Gradually, as vocabulary increases, an adult again. But a different adult. Who am I, then, that language can so change me? What is personality, identity? And the deeper change, the profounder understanding—partial, at least—of what man is, devoid of words. Where could wordlessness lead? Shocks, insights, astounding and sudden walls. Equally astounding and sudden dematerializations; points of view shifting and vanishing. Attitudes recognized for what they are: attitudes. The Word behind the word...but when there is no word...?

("Why did you stop writing?" "I didn't. It stopped." "Nonsense, you're the master." "Am I?") Who would not, after all, be a poet, a good poet, if one could choose? If one could choose. Most of one's life one has the illusion of choice. And when that is removed, when clearly one cannot choose... Blank page after blank page. The thing I had feared most of all had happened at last. This time I never would write again. But by some combination of factors—coincidence, serendipity—the pen that had written was now, most surprisingly drawing. ("Why did you start drawing?" "I didn't. It started." "But why start something you know nothing about and chuck up all the techniques and skills...?") Why, indeed, why? What was that tiny fret, that wordless dizzying vibration, the whole molecular dance? Is that what Tobey's white writing wrote? What was that golden shimmer, the bright pink shine on the anturias, the delicately and exactly drawn design of the macaw's feathers? Why did I suddenly see with the eye of an ant? Or a fly? The golden—yes, there it was again—web spun by the spider among the leaves of the century plant? Surely the very purpose of a web demands invisibility? Yet this was a lure, a glistening small sun, jewelled already with opalescent victims. Victims of what?

The impotence of a marmoset in a rage, pitting itself against me, its fingers like the stems of violets, unable to break the skin of my hand. How quickly one learns about scale with a marmoset for companion. Man in a rage with his gods, or, equally superficially, pleased with them. The glorious macaw, the flesh of his Groucho Marx face wrinkled and soft, his crazy hilarious laughter and low seductive chuckles making him kin until one looked into his infinitely dilatable eye and was drawn through its vortex into a minute cosmos which contained all the staggering dimensions of outer space.

I wonder now if "brazil" would have happened wherever I was? As to where it pointed I hadn't the least idea, nor, I think, did I ask any questions beyond the immediate ones. But I drew as if my life depended on it—each tile of each house, each leaf of each tree, each blade of grass, each mote of sunlight—all things bright and beautiful. If I drew them all...? And I did. Compelled, propelled by the point of my pen. And in drawing them all I seemed to make them mine, or make peace with them, or they with me. And then, having drawn everything—each drop of water and grain of sand—the pen began dreaming. It began a life of its own.

Looking back with my purely psychological eye through the long clear topaz of that day, I appear as a mute observer, an inarticulate listener, occupying another part of myself.

If Brazil was day, then Mexico was night. All the images of darkness hovered for me in the Mexican sunlight. If Brazil was a change of place, then Mexico was a change of time. One was very close to the old gods here. Death and the old gods. Their great temples rose all around one. Temples to the Sun. Temples to the Moon.

Objects dissolved into their symbols. All the pyramids and stairs, plumed serpents in stone, masks of jade, obsidian knives, skulls of crystal—or sugar.

In the rain forest stood the bone-white ruins of buildings—tangible remains of a whole mythology. Buildings so intricate—(tarsal, metatarsal)—

one was tempted to believe they were skeletons from which the flesh had long since rotted. Motionless. Beautiful. Great ivory kings and queens beneath their lacy cranial combs. Palaces and gardens of the Sleeping Beauty.

The villages seemed unchanged since the beginning of time. The same adobe huts, the same fields of maize, the same ancient languages of clicking consonants, and surely, the same gods Gods hungry for human blood. (Too much Lowry and Lawrence?) The plazas of Catholic churches were stages for the old rituals of costumed dances, stamped out to the music of conch shell and drum.

In Oaxaca the women of Yalalag wear triple crosses which led Cortés's priests to the mistaken belief that Christian missionaries had preceded them. Oaxacans perhaps understand the symbolism of the cross: time passing, time eternal—"the intersection of this world with eternity." In Chichén Itzá the Carocol or Snail—an observatory dome from which the Mayans probed the heavens—has four small openings exactly pointing to the cardinal directions. Temples of the Cross. Temples of the Foliated Cross.

Coming as I do from a random or whim-oriented culture, this recurrence and interrelating of symbols into an ordered and significant pattern—prevalent too in the folk arts of pottery and weaving—was curiously illuminating. One did not feel restricted by the enclosed form of the "design"; rather, one was liberated into something life-giving and larger. I could now begin to understand how the "little world is created according to the prototype of the great world."

Great or little, for me it was still a night world—one into which the pattern was pricked like a constellation—bright, twinkling, hard to grasp, harder still to hold. A dreaming world in which I continued to draw and to dream. How to make a noumenal doll; how to fly; the man with one black and one white hand—(Hari-Hara?); Osiris—(The Seat of the Eye); the room with the invisible walls; the circular dance beside the sea—(Initiation? Into what? A non-religious Christian? a religious non-Christian?) Poetry was more than ever now in the perceiving. My only access to it was through the dream and the drawing.

I had my first two shows during this period. The age of my graphic innocence was past. I had acquired another mask, another label. Each additional one seemed to move me further from my own centre. I was now suddenly and sharply reminded of the young Rilke, bored on a rainy afternoon, coming upon the clothing and paraphernalia of disguise in the wardrobes of a spare room; and how, masked, turbaned and cloaked, he had struck a pose before a mirror. "I stared," he wrote, "at this great, terrifying unknown personage before me and it seemed appalling to me that I should be alone with him."

Which is the mask and which the self? How distinguish, let alone separate, two such seemingly interpenetrating matters? As if pursued by the Hound of Heaven I raced back and forth among the *Collected Works* of Jung, *The Perennial Philosophy, The Doors of Perception,* Zen, C.S. Lewis, St. John of the Cross.

"See how he who thinks himself one is not one, but seems to have as many personalities as he has moods."

"Understand that thou thyself art even another little world, and hast within thee the sun and the moon, and also the stars..."

I began to suspect, in what would once have been near-heresy, that drawing and writing were not only ends in themselves, as I had previously thought, but possibly the means to an end which I could barely imagine—a method, perhaps, of tracing the "small design." And the very emergence of these ideas began to clear a way, remove the furniture and provide a new space.

But when something one has thought opaque appears translucent, transparent even, one questions whether it might not ultimately become entirely invisible. Solid walls dissolved disconcertingly into scrims. For the moment I was uncertain where to lean.

The dark Mexican night had led me back into myself and I was startlingly aware of the six directions of space.

A day and a night had passed. My return to Canada, if the pattern continued, should be the start of a new day.

The culture shock of homecoming after many years abroad is even greater, I think, than the culture shock of entering a new country. One returns different, to a different place, misled by the belief that neither has changed. Yet I am grateful for the shocks. The conditioning process which turns live tissue into fossil is arrested by the earthquake. Even buried strata may be exposed.

I had a small retrospective show shortly after coming home, followed by the publication of a book of "retrospective" poetry. The shutting of twin doors. Not necessarily on drawings and poems but on those drawings and those poems.

The questions had now become more pressing than the images. Some of the questions were retrospective: had the move from writing to drawing been a return to the primitive in myself—to the "first man" of Van der Post? Was it a psychological starting again from the pre-verbal state? If in the life of the individual and the life of the race, drawing precedes written literature, was this step back really a beginning? Certainly the varied scenes through which I had journeyed had provided no lack of subject matter.

More urgent, however, were the questions raised by Alan McGlashan: "Who or what is the Dreamer within us? To whom is the Dreamer talking? What, indeed, is this duologue, so like an effortless poem? Can projected images be manifested as dreams? Are all dreams projected? Or some? Is the Dreamer active or passive? Initiator or recipient? Sometimes one, sometimes the other? And what about the waking Dreamer? Are thoughts the invisible dreams of a daylight world? Projected by what, or whom? Jung's collective unconscious? Rumi's angels?

I don't know the answers to these questions but merely posing them moves more furniture. I begin to sense another realm—interrelated—the high doh of a scale in which we are the low. And in a sudden and momentary bouleversement, I realize that I have been upside down in life—like a tree on its head, roots exposed in the air.

The question of the mask which confronted me with such violence in Mexico has subtly shifted. In our popcorn packages when I was a child, along with the tin rings, jacks, marbles and other hidden surprises, one was occasionally lucky enough to find a small coloured picture complete with strips of transparent red and green celluloid. The picture, viewed alone, was of a boy with an umbrella and a dog. Seen through the green filter, the umbrella disappeared. The red filter demolished the dog. My subconscious evidently knew something about the tyranny of subjectivity years ago when it desired to go "through to the area behind the eyes/where silent, unrefractive whiteness lies." I didn't understand the image then but it arrived complete. It was not to be denied even though only half-glimpsed, enigmatic. It's pleasant now to know what I was talking about!

Whether or not the handful of poems written recently means that writing has "started" again, I do not know; whether there is any advance over earlier work, I shall have to let others decide. For the time being my primary concern is to remove the filters.

Meanwhile the images have begun again and the questions continue.

"What do I sing and what does my lute sing?"

*Reprinted from *The Glass Air: Poems Selected and New* (OUP 1991).

Ajmer Rode

AJMER RODE'S first book, *Vishva Di Nuhar,* dealt with the theory of relativity in dialogue form inspired by Plato's *Republic.* It was published by the Punjabi University, Punjab, India in 1966, the year he immigrated to Canada. He attended the University of Waterloo, Ontario, completing his M.A. Sc. degree in 1968. Since then he has been living on the West Coast writing both in English and Punjabi. He has published four books of poetry including *Blue Meditations* (Third Eye) and *Poems on My Doorstep* (Caitlin) in English and the other two in Punjabi. In 1994, Ajmer was given the Best Overseas Punjabi Writer Award by the Punjab Government. Comments Punjabi critic, Dr. Attar Singh: "Ajmer has quietly extended the boundaries of the Punjabi language and has given a new turn to Punjabi poetry." *Dooja Passa* and *Komagata Maru* are his books of Punjabi plays. His latest unpublished play, *Nirlajj,* on the issue of gender selection, has been produced several times over the past two years. He has written and directed nine plays and is considered a founder of Canadian Punjabi theatre. Rode has translated Gurdial Singh's outstanding Punjabi novel, *Marhi Da Diva,* into English *(The Last Flicker);* and a selection of Michael Bullock's poems, *101 Surrealist Poems,* from English to Punjabi. Guru Nanak Dev University, India, honoured him with the "Prominent Citizen's (literature) Award" in 1994 and GN Engg. College, the same year, honoured him with the "Poet of Life Award." Since 1994, he has been writing full time after leaving an engineering position with B.C. Gas. He lives with his wife, Surjeet Kalsey, daughter, Surti, and son, Ankurneel in Vancouver.

In Blue Meditation

I

In blue meditation
she smiled
in muse
she spoke:

this moment
I shall become a river
and flow into you
this moment
I shall flood.
the next moment
is yours
gush out into a spring
evaporate drop by drop.
it is your will.

the next moment.
I must go
barriers of love and earth
shall wash.

II

In blue meditation
she smiled
in muse
she spoke:

in the eyes of this tree
I wake
in its lakes
I sleep
if you are born
a leaf on this tree
I am your destiny.
walk if you can
walk down the branches
to the root
walk to the bough
in the sky

I wait for you everywhere.

III

Transcend
the layers of Maya
stand naked
once
in blue meditation

a sun shall walk
into your forehead
and dissolve.

a glow will touch
the umber of your eyes
and radiate.

Ancestral Museum

My meditations
centre on the island
infinitely small
somewhere
in the vast universe
of my chromosomes.

the island
in absolute rest
surrounded by a pool
of silence
is a museum of
ancestral images, dreams
metaphors and writings
with enormous detail

when here, my spirit
relaxes at the pool
and continues adding
to the ancestral treasure
travelling from
generation to generation

when
after external wanderings
my spirit returns
in suffering,
it writes everything in blue,
private, not a part
of the ancestral material

the day my spirit fails to return
the writings in blue
will be discarded
along with my body

yet my spirit goes on
recording
with ever more
ferocity in blue,
deeper, unknown

only a fraction is
accessible to my
blue meditations.

That Name

on atoms of the absolute darkness
when I try to write that name
words of different tongues
crowd my hand

in moments of absolute silence
when I try to utter that name
notes emerging at random
choke my voice

in desperation I return
to my mundane world
and wait again
for the absolute
hoping to record the name
that walks in me
from cell to cell

with no aim.

ਅੰਤਰ ਲਿਸ਼ਕੋਰ

ਕਲ੍ਹ ਜੋ ਤਾਰਾ ਅੱਧੀ ਰਾਤੀਂ
ਅੰਬਰਾਂ ਵਿਚੋਂ ਤੁਰਿਆ
ਅਜ ਅਚਾਨਕ ਮਸਤਕ ਅੰਦਰ
ਟੋਟੇ ਟੋਟੇ ਹੋਇਆ
ਕਣ ਕਣ ਚਾਨਣ ਕਣ ਸੰਗ ਮਿਲਿਆ
ਚਾਨਣ ਚਾਨਣ ਚਾਨਣ
ਕੁਝ ਚਾਨਣ ਮੈਂ ਓਸੇ ਖਿਣ ਹੀ
ਰੰਗਾਂ ਵਿਚ ਡਬੋਇਆ

ਕੁਝ ਚਾਨਣ ਮੈਂ ਕੋਸਾ ਕੋਸਾ
ਤੈਨੂੰ ਅਰਪਨ ਕੀਤਾ
ਕੁਝ ਚਾਨਣ ਮੈਂ ਠੰਢਾ ਠੰਢਾ
ਮਾਂ ਦੀ ਅੱਖ ਸਮੋਇਆ
ਕੁਝ ਚਾਨਣ ਮੈਥੋਂ ਅੰਦਰੇ ਅੰਦਰ
ਸੁਰਤੀ ਚੋਰੀ ਕੀਤਾ
ਕੁਝ ਚਾਨਣ ਮੇਰੇ ਨੈਣੀਂ ਬਹਿ ਕੇ
ਅੱਥਰੂ ਅਥਰੂ ਰੋਇਆ

ਕੁਝ ਚਾਨਣ ਗਲ ਬਾਹਾਂ ਪਾ ਕੇ
ਰੂਹ ਮੇਰੀ ਸੰਗ ਸੁੱਤਾ
ਬਾਕੀ ਚਾਨਣ ਖਿਣ ਨ ਰੁਕਿਆ
ਕਿਰਨਾਂ ਕਿਰਨਾਂ ਹੋਇਆ ॥

Still Light

The star
that vanished from
the sky at midnight
burst in my forehead
at twilight
filling me
with the still light

some light I immersed
in colours right away
some light with a bit
of sun in it I gave away.
some light with
a bit of cool dawn
I put in the eyes of my mother
some light
with a bit of blue in it
I stole for myself

some light sat in my eyes
and wept
some light put arms
around me and slept

rest of the light
not another moment stayed
became all rays

Heart of the Seed

in the forest
I found the seed
that sprouted into the entire forest.
in the seed
I set forth to reach
the point
where growth of the seed
first began.

The instant I reached,
I spread over the entire forest.

Stroll in a Particle

if you can find
a path into it
there is enough
space in this
particle
to stroll a lifetime.

Knock Gently

knock gently
when you reach the cottage
of my soul.
the door shall fling open
a flood of light shall
wash your tired feet.

Yellow Smile

Every morning
I sell myself to the
same master and
stay shut in his cage
for eight hours.

lest I should join
ranks of the dead
my spirit accompanies me
in the cage.

in the evening
when I return to myself
I look into the eyes
of my spirit and say:
let us fly.
my wings are too tired
replies the spirit with
a yellow smile

together we mourn
the death of another day

The Maharishi and the Baby

The maharishi whispers:
the flesh is maya
the soul is eternal,
the truth.

the baby
inside a starved mother
insists it must come out
the mother must eat.

the maharishi
and the baby in the womb
stare across
into each other's eyes.

Guru and the Lotus Eyes

The lotus-eyed woman
who came to Aristotle was
wrapped in serene beauty.
Fragrance spread as she spoke:

Guru, speak to me the essence
of being.

Aristotle smiled and said:
I am I and you are you,
I am not you and you are not me,
that is all you need to know.

Oh, that is simple, guru,
that was ever clear to me
as a bird song.

Bird songs sound complicated to me
said Aristotle.
Their patterns
their meanings...
I wish I could understand them.

But I do, I really do said the woman.
Bird songs resonate with the
songs my soul whispers
every evening,
tell me something deeper,
something I can dive into again and again.

That is all I can tell you at the
moment and I believe
it will usher a new era in human
thinking, said the guru,
impressed by the woman's
grace and her interest.
Holding her hand in his hand
he continued,
let us make a deal. You have free
access to my intellect,

with all its truths and no-truths.
In turn let me resonate
with your soul that resonates
with bird songs.

But then, said the woman,
I will be I and I will be you,
You will be you and you will be I.
This could usher yet another era
in human relations.

Rubbish. This sounds so dialectical. Rubbish,
said Aristotle,
still holding the woman's hand in
his hand.

There was a long silence. The
time ticked on, confused.

Playing with Big Numbers

The human mind
is essentially qualitative.
As you know,
we are easily excited by pinks
and purples, triangles and circles
and we are ever
confused over
true and false,
right and wrong.

But quantitative analyses rarely
touch our souls.

Numbers were invented mainly
by men to trick each other.
I am almost certain women
had nothing to do with
them. They had more
vital tasks like survival
at hand.

But playing with big numbers
could be interesting.
In fact it could be really
fun. Say if I were
to sit on a gravel pit and count
one billion pebbles non-stop
it will take me some 14 years;
or if I were to count what Africa
owes to rich
foreigners—some 200 billion
dollars,
it is impossible. I will have to
be born 40 times and do nothing
but keep counting 24 hours.

Although things could be simpler on a
smaller scale. Suppose as a result
of the debt, five million children die
every year, as in fact they do,
and each dying child cries
a minimum of 100 times a day
there would be a trillion cries
floating around
in the atmosphere just over a
period of five years.
Remember a sound wave once
generated never ceases to exist
in one form or the other,
and never escapes
the atmosphere.

Now one fine morning, even if
one of these cries suddenly hits
you, it will shatter your soul into
a billion pieces. It will take
14 years to gather
the pieces and put them back
into one piece.

On the other hand, maybe all the
trillion cries could hit your soul
and nothing would happen.

Take My Hands

Take my two hands
make eight feet of them
give them to the spider I
soaked in hot water in
my kitchen sink. Accidentally.
I will hide my arms
in long sleeves, will
finish the last painting with
brush in my teeth
but take my two hands.
If the spider,
motionless as a
cold stone, dies
she will weave her next web
in my soul
will travel with me
through all the lives
eighty four thousand
and more.

Ajmer Rode
An Essay

Spirituality for me eludes definition, even though I use the word often and like the response it evokes. Awareness of the mysterious in its immensity, as well as in the unknown element that lurks behind every little thing, comes closest to my sense of the sacred. The most beautiful thing I have experienced as a writer is the mystery of a creative urge. When such an urge takes hold of me, I reach for the nearest pen, the nearest paper lying around and start scribbling. I don't ask: what is this urge? Where did it come from? I simply obey, with the maximum speed my hand can move at. Later on I may go to the keyboard, rewrite, revise, extend, edit. Later on I may spend hours on something I initially got in a flash, in a minute or two. Too often the creative urge loses its vitality when a mind overpopulated with past thinking, diction and devices tries to give expression to it. I envy those who can receive and reshape creative impulses with relatively free minds, like the poets who created the Vedas, the first sacred texts of India, four thousand years ago.

The Vedic poets, or the Rishies as they were called, did not work out their poems laboriously; that is how the belief goes. They actually *saw* complete poems or had darshana (sacred seeing) of them and simply transcribed them. That is why they were regarded as seers. The religious faithfuls believe a divine power revealed the poems to the Rishies. Even the language of the Vedas, they believe, was given to the Rishies by the same source. But the real reason the Rishies were able to write so effortlessly would be that they actually lived what they wrote. They worshipped multiple deities: Agni, the god of fire, Indra, the god of rain, the god of wind, of night, of morning. They saw a god in every natural phenomenon. The concept of a supreme God had not originated at that time, as the Vedas themselves reveal. The Rishies' belief in the gods was real and full. If they wrote about the god of wind, they actually felt the god within and without them. If they wrote in praise of the morning, they actually felt the beautiful Usha, the goddess of the morning, touching them with her golden rays.

And the Rishies were able to see things around them differently from most of us. There were no poetics, no elaborate theories established at that time; their minds were not prisoners of long literary traditions (as Punjabi poet Dr. Haribhajan Sing notes). Every time they sat to write, their minds were ready to experience afresh; their spirits were free to cherish the new. It is not as much the content of the Vedas as the process of their creation that has influenced me. At times, rare of course, when I am able to detach myself from the tradition, able to unlearn the past, ordinary things look different, become interesting, fluid, responsive. Once the new awareness dawns, the mind follows its own path, ready to touch the untouched, taste the prohibited. Each word comes naked, excited, eager to assume a new meaning The writing effort slips to the background; the pen merely collects the unexpected gifts, the fruits that suddenly appear one after the other.

The phenomenon of awareness is a great mystery and at the centre of spirituality. When I become aware that I am aware, I feel transformed; when I become aware of others of the physical world, of the unknown, I feel liberated, extended, connected. Awareness is absolute. Instant. This moment I am aware of myself; the next, of the entire universe. Imagination is different—wonderful, but a consequence of the material. Awareness is alive, intelligent, its origin aphysical, I believe. Awareness can step out of the space-time-energy world of science and look at itself. Yet I am reluctant to attribute the source of awareness to an all-knowing supreme being. The concept of an absolute God pleased at being worshipped oppresses me. I was born into a Sikh background, have learnt much from Sikh scriptures, but do not practice Sikhism or any other religion.

Art and science, with all their well understood differences, have a lot in common. The same creative urge that fires in an artist inspires a scientist before the logical construction sets in. Science, despite its seemingly awesome power, humbly declares that its conclusions are never to be taken as the final truth. The reality described by its present set of laws is just one in a multi-reality existence. Science is a sub set, not the whole. Its transformation into abusive technology is very disturbing and devastating. But pure science also unfolds for me the beauty of the physical world.

Once, without any specific reason, I stood in the door of my house and realized that I was smaller than the door. And the door was smaller than the house and the house smaller than the earth. The earth was tiny in the solar system, the solar system in its galaxy, the galaxy in the cluster, one in millions floating in the immense universe. When I came back to myself, I was standing on an earth no larger than a zillionth of a dust particle. But I was still there, for sure, with my awareness that had saved me from a devastating sense of insignificance. But when I went the other way and saw that I was larger than my hand, my hand larger than a cell, the cell larger than an atom, the atom than an elementary particle...I got lost. I had no point to come back to. I had become a collection of a zillion blinking sub-atomic particles. This experience, not unique to me I am sure, never faded from my memory and has inspired some of my Punjabi poetry.

My poetry and other writings have also been affected by human suffering. I grew up in village poverty, have lived next to city slums and have seen people fighting over half-eaten bananas on garbage piles. World poverty is overwhelming and has etched a mark on my psyche. In North America the evil of poverty is less, but it is hard to escape the feeling of imprisonment in a system that encourages greed, competition, and shameless exploitation of the environment and humans. I believe our spirituality, our sense of the sacred, our talk of connectedness, will remain hollow if we remain stranger to the sea of human suffering that is vast and deep.

Robin Skelton

ROBIN SKELTON (1925-1997) grew up in England, and served in India and Ceylon with the R.A.F. during World War II. In 1963 he immigrated to Canada to teach at the University of Victoria, where he founded the Department of Creative Writing. A poet, anthologist, novelist, short-story writer, translator, publisher, scholar, editor, biographer, art and literary critic, and historical writer, Robin Skelton has published over 100 books. He remains a leading authority on poetic forms and the Irish drama. In his later years he was initiated into the mysteries of Wicca. His poetry collection, *The Edge of Time,* was nominated for the 1996 B.C. Book Prize for Poetry. He passed away in August of 1997, leaving a number of substantial works still to be released.

Everything

Everything is in the light of everything, holy.
But do not expect a catalogue of grace,
trees, leaves, grass, and children suddenly shouting
Hi-Hi, loudly, running in their playground
for to select is always to leave out something
quiet, unnoticed, like the snail shell lying
under the black and rotten bit of the gatepost,
or the swing of the signature on the paper,
all of a movement. Everything is moving
in its own direction, sure as owls
dipping the blind hedges, the small stone walls,
in the stiff hills where everything keeps house
within the sound of wind, each, any stirring
slowly towards itself, defeat and conquest,
end and beginning meaningless, arrival
only a word to stand for somewhere else
imbued with what we are more than ourselves.
And this we must remember: every thing
is, before everything, holy and astir
with an unfolding plenitude we are
the heirs and bequeathers to our sons.
Therefore be thankful when you thank; be sure
when time assures you on the dragging path;
be kind when you are kindred; do not lend
uncertainties to strangers or take truth
away from anyone, but still be still
in movement and in peace, the language turning
always upon your silence. Look around.
Everything, before everything, is yours
and none an island—no, none, none, not one
but is the others'. We possess ourselves
only so far as others lean to us
and draw us, moving, into their stirred house
as easily as air, only so far
as everything remains itself and sings.

The Rule
for Ludwig Zeller

There is a rule
applicable to children—

which we should not
at any time forget.

Thus, when a bull's
discovered in the garden

or a unicorn
ascends the stairs,

we must not call the
wide-eyed tale a lie

or even speak about
imagination,

but accept realities;
we, too,

see what we do not see
and cannot know.

Knowledge

Knowledge does not arrive
by studied labour;

though you hunch year on
year above your books

and Bachelor, Master, Doctor
of each science,

labour farther to
enlarge your mind,

you cannot come to
knowledge; that eludes

deliberate effort as
does ecstasy,

and must happen
suddenly, your startled

understanding falling
to its knees.

Sanctuary

It is a sanctuary. I stared
at the sand,
at the eggs
in the small hollow,

suddenly scared at my
wish. Terns.
I heard it "turns"
and felt a turning

in me somewhere,
a slow curve
coming round
without an end

or a beginning,
a single turn
I must not touch.
I knew the law:

Don't touch the eggs,
disturb the birds.
I felt that I
disturbed the birds;

they were so quick
and light and went
away and something
other went

away in them.
Now, come away.
I came away.
I came away,
and yet I stayed

with that curve in my
mind, that sense
of swerve, of
untouched altering,

which, like the law,
I still protect,
and, too, that frightening
sanctuary.

Lost

for Kathleen Raine

Only the lost poem tells
the story true,

the poem that slipped
into a crack in time

and is now a wing that
never flew,

a hand that never touched,
a throat that strained

for speech but never spoke,
could not arrange

the cloak of language round
the naked light.

from "*Words for Witches*"

Names

Do not use too many names,
for names

are separations,
and we all are one

in past and present;
names reverberate

particulars till the
unity is drowned

in vast obliquities
of sound and image;

rather speak of
Her without a name,

of Him without a name,
retaining thus

the rhythm of the breath:
Her Him, Her Him,

Her Him, Her Him, Her Him,
our endless music.

The Witches

When we were cursed
we versed ourselves in tidals.

When we were bound
we found ropes reached the sky.

When we were racked
we hooked our hands on mountains.

When we were burned
we learned that life is flame.

And when they said
that we were dead, we bled

into the rain that feeds us all,
and called

ourselves the future,
seeking farther, farther,

and we were born
again, again, again....

To My Sons and Daughters

I have been talking to you for fifty years.
I started long before you were even born,
wanting to show you clearly who I am.
It is sometimes hard to rest unknown
within the language even while I spin
more filaments, believing I'll catch your eye
some day with this dexterity or that,
knowing, however, that only when I die
will this cocoon be broken, and for a brief
inexpressible moment I will be
not what I am but what I am become
and unfamiliar still to you who see
the slow increasing swathes and do not know
what they contain and hide, only aware
of something happening that you half admire
and half distrust.
                Love brings its own despair,
and I despair, unable to break through
the fine-spun circumstance, for no life does
without destruction or a transformation
from mankind into something more than man.
So what am I to do? I'd speak more plain,
spin clear transparent fibres if I could,
but it's too late; I've been obscured too long

and have no hopes of being understood
the way I wish, the way we all wish,
spinning, spinning, separate and alone,
however loving and however loved,
all knowing that we can but rest unknown
to all save that companion we call
God, Goddess, Angel, Deity, who sees
within whatever lives the life itself
and hears the words, and hears beyond the words.

Tao
(Catena Rondo)
for Pat Martin Bates

Because it is an empty room,
the windows brilliant with light,
the walls of white, the ceiling white;
because it is an empty room

the windows brilliant with light,
I stand within it, still and tall,
white blazing ceiling floor and wall,
the windows brilliant with light.

I stand within it, still and tall,
waiting for the secret name,
the moment incandescent flame;
I stand within it, still and tall,

waiting for the secret name,
a name that answers every call
and every question, healing all
waiting for the secret name,

a name that answers every call
because it is an empty room
devoid of why or whence or whom,
a name that answers every call

because it is an empty room,
the windows brilliant with light,
the walls of white, the ceiling white
because it is an empty room.

The Process

Begin with listening—the voice
elsewhere and here, a gleam of brown,
its movements fluent and its flying leaps
the sudden judgement of a heart in shock
at precipices we'd not thought to find.

It spills through time, and aeon on aeon grow
within it, history a grace-note held
a hundredth of a second; it enfolds
earth, sky and water, and is magma, centre,
and the trembling of a single hair,

and it begins where there is no beginning
and no end. It is not of the spheres
or of the gods of some angelic host;
it is the all we cannot ever know
and yet become as we become ourselves.

Finally

So much is gone. But where? What's lost,
abandoned, set aside, must yet exist
as under towns the strata, layer on layer
down to the magma fire. Raising ghosts
is what I'm doing maybe, thinking up
the scarred and wooden desk, the cracked
porcelain inkwell—yet they come unbidden
as does the garden roller splashed with grass
and the bitter sloes in the ragged hedgerow.
All that was is here somewhere, but if
I spent my life recovering my life
it well might take another lifetime, and
what would be the point? To find, to know
the sharpened sense, the friend's young face, her sudden
startled eyes, a feather in a roadway,
a new book, that first fingering of a leaf
how could one, arms crammed, carry through
these final years the hoard we are become,
and would it matter we were so enriched?
Or maybe everything that's gone has gone
before us and is waiting, dross shucked off,
the hurts and harms forgotten. That is heaven
wouldn't you say? But I've no dream of heaven,
only of continuing on and on
until what comes is more than all that's gone.

An Interview with Robin Skelton (January, 1997)

SM: Quite a while ago in your book on poetics, *The Truth of Poetry* (1978), you wrote that poetry is "opposed to any dogma, fixed system, and any philosophy which tries to objectify the nature of humanity." Could you elaborate a bit on how you see poetry addressing the human need for wholeness without recurring to fixed ideological or religious structures?

RS: I think that in the Western tradition, the problem is solved by being, as a matter of fact, narcissistic or autobiographical, because the only wholeness we have a chance of grasping is our own. Therefore, writing personal lyrics is not necessarily avoiding the issue. This is really a kind of Shelleyian position, or even a Yeatsian position. But that's what I think, on the whole. I don't object to poets who follow a particular philosophy, or line, or religion, but my own personal view is that none of my poems fits any religion.

SM: Many, I would say most, of the poets in the anthology, for whatever reasons, perhaps because of my personal preferences or because of the nature of poetry itself, don't seem to fit into any kind of orthodox schema. They seem to be either pushing the boundaries, or completely outside conventional religion.

RS: Yes, I think that's true. There are, of course, Catholic poets, profoundly Catholic poets. And that seems to be the only western religion that seems to have adherents who produce poems along the given party line. But even those are sometimes a little bit dodgy in terms of orthodoxy.

SM: Your work is eclectic, ranging through a variety of spiritual traditions, both eastern and western, and through a variety of related poetic forms from Haiku to meditative verse to spells. Yet your interest in pre-Christian Celtic myth and ritual has led you into a serious embracing of Wicca as evidenced in your poems "Words for Witches." Can you speak briefly about your interest in Wicca and its place in your work?

RS: Wicca came to me out of a very gradual development in my searching around things and writing about things, and generally messing about. But it is none the less sincere for that. I arrived at it. Whether it's the last thing I'll arrive at, I'm not about to say, because I don't know. But I had previously read a good deal of stuff on other religions, and, as you say, I had done a lot of work on different forms, different traditions. I've now done all the Japanese forms, which is more than you will find in other reference books. I've also written in all the Welsh forms, and all the Irish ones. While I'm interested in the Oriental, I'm also very interested in the Celtic. I am, after all, one-eighth Celt myself. The witchcraft I use is in the Celtic tradition.

SM: So did this interest begin in England, not just after you came out to the West Coast?

RS: It began in the late fifties, but didn't develop very much until I got to Vancouver Island, where I actually met my first witch. All the others were people who had been interested, but not real witches.

SM: There's a difference between theoretical interest and actual practice. Has the practice of witchcraft changed your poetry?

RS: I don't know. I'm not the best critic of my own poetry. In fact, I try to avoid it, because I never know when I'm right or not. It may have affected it to the extent that more of my poems are short and spell-like than earlier, but I don't know whether this is true or not. As I grow older, the poems seem to grow shorter, and it seems to me appropriate.

SM: Do you make a connection between magic and poetry?

RS: Well, it depends on what you mean by magic, and if you mean by magic what I do, the use of psychic energy to change things, to change actuality, then it doesn't relate to poetry. Poetry is the use of psychic energy, but the difference between a poem and a spell is simply that the spell asserts, it doesn't permit any questioning, any riddling; whereas the poem is liable to argue against itself, and do all sorts of elaborate things. So you may get poems that are spells, or spells that are poems, whichever way round you want it, but not all poetry is going to be magic in that sense, except, of course, that just as magic depends very much on music and dance, so, in my view, poetry should depend on the spoken voice, which is music, and upon rhythm, which is dance. So I'm an old-fashioned poet who really believes in the Muse, in poetry that is song and dance.

SM: In *Memoirs of a Literary Blockhead* (1988), you speak of your practice of the healing arts as tied to the Old Religion, as well as other forms of magic. To what extent is poetry for you a healing art?

RS: I really don't know; I've never thought of that before. Yet, poetry can be self-therapy, and some poems directed at people may be attempting to heal, but I've never thought of poetry as a healing art itself. It can and does disturb; it arouses people, it makes them, perhaps, think, and does therefore have a healing quality, but I don't think of it that way. When I do healing, it's an entirely different activity.

SM: What can you say about the reaches and limitations of language? You talk about silence a lot in your poetry. Does poetry lead us up to the edge of what is unspeakable, unsayable?

RS: The kind of poetry I'm interested in does take us to that edge, but there's another kind of poetry which is linguistically complicated. Some of the new poetry tries to take language farther than I was prepared to, because I feel that we reach the edge of language which is, in a sense, silence, by speaking the words, the kind of language everybody else speaks. If we invent too many words, if we make it so complicated that nobody else can follow it, we're not doing the job. Some poets irritate me by being unnecessarily complicated or obscure. I want somebody who will speak to me directly. I like language that is clear, lucid, passionate, resonant. It shouldn't wreck the actual, usable, used syntax of the language. Let us stay roughly within syntactical bounds.

SM: In the academic world postmodernist, poststructural theory has been dominant for a while. Some forms of it seem antithetical to the old language about the soul, the spirit, silence, eternity, etc.

RS: I've never actually understood what postmodernism and poststructuralism mean, though I discovered to my surprise, I'd written quite a number of postmodern poems, but I didn't know this. Well, if you want to say the soul has no meaning, you can say the same thing about spirit or the self. We live in terms of certain vocabularies, and if we change the vocabulary, we change the way we live, which is fair enough. But then all we do is substitute another vocabulary. I choose to believe in something I call the soul; they can choose to believe in something they call the "psychic hinterland" or something. It doesn't make any difference. The "culturally constructed self" doesn't mean a damned thing, because we're all culturally constructed. I think they should go away and talk to the Aruba in West Africa, and see how that works out, or go talk to a really educated Hindu. You have to make a lot of shifts.

SM: Some of the poets I've interviewed say they don't feel comfortable with the language of "spirit" or "spirituality." Everyone has certain terms they resist and others with which they feel more comfortable. Are you saying we should not try to invent new vocabularies for the divine, but reclaim the ones we already have?

RS: No, I don't really mind. Let anybody go whatever path he or she has chosen to go. But I dislike it when people dismiss other peoples' beliefs and theories too quickly. There's a Taoist physicist (which is a nice combination) who maintained that we are going to die and go to whatever we imagined, which is an interesting thought. I think he also maintained something about the soul, saying, in effect, that the soul is the word you use or don't use. But I can't get too excited about these "isms"; they come in and they go out, and they enable a number of academics to make a lot of money by writing articles about them.

SM: Some poets now are writing out of the apophatic tradition, where naming, labels, concepts have to be relinquished, and the poet enters a "cloud of unknowing" in which letting go of names is part of the process.

RS: If that's the way you want to go, that's the way you go. I've written poems recently about letting go. I don't habitually name God in my poems, or even the Goddess (whom I believe in even more). But you see, the problem with the "Cloud of Unknowing," as a term, is the problem of communication. I don't really know what it means. One of the things I always feel about writing, writing a poem even, and I feel this profoundly is, "Can you photograph it?" If you can't photograph it, think again, which sounds as if one is wholly dependent upon imagism, but that's really not what I mean at all. I want the clarity of image, particularly if it's a crucial image.

SM: Yes, often so-called "spiritual poetry" can become very abstract.

RS: Then it needs the sound. If you get really abstract, you really need metre, you need rhythm, you need rhyme, because then you provide the physical element by the nature of the song and dance. Then the language itself may be abstract, but the mood, the feeling, the emotion, these are there, and strongly there.

SM: Do you think that this element I'm calling the spiritual in poetry is going to have any kind of a resurgence?

RS: I'm really not sure. One problem we have is that the general level of poetry being written in Canada at the moment is really not very high. In my view, there's an enormous amount of very boring free verse. And I call it free verse out of charity, because it's mostly just prose sawed up into lengths. And it is very tedious. And very little of it has any subject matter that interests me except anecdotes about people's lives and their love lives (which only interest me when they become erotic). Really! I think something should happen and perhaps it will.

SM: Do you think there is some current of Canadian poetry dealing with more profound subject matter?

RS: I suppose there is. I'm really not so completely clued into what poetry is doing here at the minute. I remember visiting Robert Graves in his study, and he had practically no books by anybody else, and not even all his own. He just didn't want to get confused by reading somebody else's work when he was trying to do his own. There's an enormous quantity being published now, and I think this is excellent, but an awful lot of boring poetry gets printed. But, of course, a lot of boring other books get printed as well, so you can't really complain too much. What I do find really distressing is that you produce a book of poetry, even a big one like a collected poems of somebody, and the press pays no attention to it. Poets are being edged out. It's not the first time, but I find it frustrating when you write poems, and can't be sure people are going to hear them.

This may seem a digression from the spiritual, but it isn't really, because one of the things you're doing when you're exploring the spiritual is trying to find a truth you want to tell somebody. A truth you keep to yourself when you're a writer is not a truth at all. I want to tell people things.

SM: Do you think the materialism of our culture crowds out poetry?

RS: There is, I think, a need for art, poetry, music to deal with problems of what we call loosely, spirituality, and to have a sense of a spiritual journey, or if you will, a psychic journey. I think it is important that we recognize this. Whether it is being crowded out by materialism or not in our culture, I'm not sure, because I've been noticing lately, on the television and other places, little signs that people are getting tired of pure materialism. They want to move ahead; they want to move forward, and I think this is likely to happen, because people are getting bored really. Boredom is a great renewer.

SM: In Dante, isn't there a sense that Hell, which he called *Ulro*, is ultimately boring?

RS: I think heaven would be enormously tedious.

SM: Well, at least the popular conception of heaven, which poets like Blake satirized, is boring. Blake's idea of heaven, which he called "eternity" in his later works, was very much more energetic though.

RS: Ah, Blake is wonderful! Blake should be read by everybody, including people who do interviews, because remember, he said that "to generalize is to be an idiot." [laughter]

SM: Oh, yes, I have to agree with him on that. And I'm going to end on that note, even if at this interviewer's expense. Thanks so much, Robin.

ANNE SZUMIGALSKI

ANNE SZUMIGALSKI was born in London, England and immigrated to Saskatoon, Saskatchewan in 1951. She is a founding member of the Saskatoon Writer's Guild and *Grain* magazine. Her 14 books include collections of poems, essays and short stories, as well as plays, and words for dance. Her book *Voice* won the Governor General's Award in 1995. Anne has read her work in Canada, the UK and USA, and in many other parts of the world. Her work has been translated into six languages. She is also a translator and is at present engaged with Elisabet Ráfols-Saquès in translating modern plays from Catalan. She has collaborated with Terrence Heath and other writers, choreographers and artists. Her drawings have been shown in several exhibitions across the country. Works for dance include *Litany of the Bagladies,* which was performed at Dance Canada, and several shorter pieces. Her play Z was produced by Twenty-fifth Street Theatre, Saskatoon in Spring 1994. Recent books include: *On Glassy Wings: Poems New and Selected* (Coteau, 1997) and a new collection of short essays and drawings, *Sermons on Stones: Words and Images* (Hagios 1997).

Woman Reading in Bath

I am swimming alone on the dark sea
When before me looms up the great stout chin of god
Floating on the black chops of the high tide
And his hands are clutching the slippery wet sides

The edges and the hems of his bungled universe

What's this curling murderously around my neck?
What's this strangling over the blue knots of my neck?
Wiry fingers of hair thick knuckle-bladders
It is a long curled lock from the godhead
Red as sargassum

When the eye is shut then shall the great globe dim
Like a popped bulb scattering flakes
Of slowly falling volcano glass round
The vast bulges of softly swimming belly
And does the great thumping creator's heart
Somehow sit inside and direct the traffic
Of sharks and seals and obedient shoals?
Lucky and cunning from the dark I watch
The huge mouthful of deified teeth from which
Squeaks out a puny cry meant to be a roar
Great heave of the chest but yet a breath
So small it hardly blows my hair about
As I tread water in the shallows
Under the square shadow of his shoulders
He heaves up on stick legs like a fat bird
Crack crack the shanks have snapped
And down he flops on the shingles gasping and stranded

I—the Director—pick up the phone
Connecting me to the sky and the undersea silt
I say *Birds come down from the clouds*
I say *Great crabs come up from the deep*
Chew on this mass—feed all your children
On it for a year

Oh what a dry and brittle skeleton he makes
But on the last day a small bone hand shall creep
Out of the gray shore sand
And grasping a pebble throw it over my head
Into deep water

Angels

have you noticed
how they roost in trees?
not like birds
their wings fold the other way

mother, whose eyes are clouding
gets up early to shoo them
out of her pippin tree
afraid they will let go their droppings
over the lovely olive
of the runnelled bark

she keeps a broom by the door
brushes them from the branches
not too gently
go and lay eggs she admonishes

they clamber down
jump clumsily to the wet ground
while she makes clucking noises
to encourage them to the nest

does not notice how they
bow down low before her anger
each lifting a cold and rosy hand
from beneath the white feathers
raising it in greeting
blessing her and the air
as they back away into the mist

Jerusalem

that city of glass these words are printed in the book that lies open before you I'm reading over your shoulder and cannot see your face but I know that your slightly bulging eyes blue as glass are staring at the page I know that from between those eyes the thought darts out and hits the print with its point that never again will you enter jerusalem

send me I want to tell you but you hush me with the warmth of your hand which is resting on my hand am I cooling your fingers or are you warming mine this question occurs at the same time as conjectures about my journey to that place of iron doors and minarets lighted against the sky whose gates are closed until morning

whose walls are huge blocks of traprock says the book where men in black homburgs weep and wail their tears run down their faces, run down the stones leaving long ribbons of rust

soon I shall scale these walls and enter the city
and search up and down the streets for those
whose names were once known to you will they
put on a false front of flesh will they come shaved
and powdered to greet me

or when at last I see them face to face will they
turn quickly away and hurry down a sidestreet
while one explains to the other a new process for
adding gold to the glass of an office building *it's
true* he admits that the windows shine rather
dully in the sun but then the people inside never
have to pull down the blinds for in that place
there is neither glitter nor glare but always just
enough light to read by

A Closed Room

/in a closed room a girl holds up an apple to the
light/notices the slanting stem/the streaky blush
that stripes the skin/this is a time of recollection
she says biting into the words/she reads them in
a book of hours/in a closed room the young girl
holds an apple up against the light/she stares at
the slanted stem/the streaky blush that stripes the
skin in this time of recollection/she reads from a
book of hours/sunbars pierce the dusty glass/
the book lies open/light bleaches the print/she
touches the slanted green stem with her finger/
opens the book of hours where the sun can slant
across it/she flings away the core opens the
creaking window/there is an orchard outside/the
trees are leafless/the girl holds an apple to the
light/the book is a book of hours/sunlight erases
the print/the girl closes the book/this is a time of
recollection she says/the girl has an apple in her

slight fingers/she holds it against the light slant-
ing through the streaky panes/she bites into the
words/the book lies open in the bleaching light/
this is a time of recollection/these words are
printed on the dusty page/the core hangs in the
air/it floats to the floorboards/it floats through
the closed window/the casement cannot be opened
/the bar is rusted to the nub/the girl wants to
throw away the core of the streaky apple she is
biting/the book will not close/the print speaks/
the girl bites into the bleached apple/she swallows
the flesh/

Annwfn

for T.H.

a world in the shape of an egg
lies in the palm of the hand

which warms it and the warmth
brings out the sheen of the eggshell

you stare at its wholeness which you know
is present only from moment to moment

in your other hand in a nest of worn fingers
lies another egg which you see as exactly like

the first but the fingers know the difference
for this one is withdrawn from its chalky shell

into its chill yolk   cannot
be warmed at a touch

god hold me to myself you cry out departing
not comprehending how you will pass through

that wall thin as eggshell to where
everything seems exactly as it was at home

yet there is a difference
if only you could put your hand on it

in the morning the farmwife comes from the house
her apron full of wheat

or what passes for wheat until the sun
hits it and it sparkles   handfuls

of crystals thrown up never to fall
while the silly hens gobble at nothing

and the young woman erased for a moment
by the dazzle of the sun

turns and becomes that other girl
rosy and solid whom you left years ago

The Compassion

the compassion of the one whose residence is a speck
of dust a grain of sand or salt the bubble of spit on
the lip of the dying   the one who has led us to
believe that the word is short almost square it might
be *come* or *go* or *desire* but nothing longer than that

a drop of rain falls into the ocean and we are com-
manded to recognize this one globule as separate
from all the rest by its freshness perhaps or by its
shape which like the planet's is spherical but imper-
fectly so

air surrounds us then the canopy of ozone which
angels pierce as they ascend from the tangent plane
at any of the possible angles   how hard it is to see
them as they dart through the tunnel of our sight

harder still to perceive their descent their legs slight-
ly parted the ball of each pale foot poised over that
house of many rooms whose windows look out on
every acre of dirt whether it is desert or forest or
a place we have laid out for ourselves a garden full
of birds and worms and creeping plants which
promised on their seed packets to flower, we be-
lieved them and have been disappointed   yet by
faith we see buds as the angels who are god's pupils
see us

$i^2 = -1$

A chocolate egg is made by binding two equal halves together.

When it is whole, balance it on the pointed end and spin. Eventually it will waver and fall on its side (but which side?) and roll. Never again will you be able to tell which half was right, and which was left.

Or indeed whether the egg is divided N/S or E/W.

But it's true, isn't it, that before something has become a whole we may not refer to it as divided? The trick of a word, the sag of the language, may mean it has always been whole, even before the two halves were joined. Apartness. Agglutination.

Invent me a set of pure symbols. Write me a letter in unmistakeable signs. But are these signs unmistake-able from each other, or are they simply unmis-takeably signs?

Now give me an imaginary number; speak me an imagined word.

Resurrection. The tomb opened. An egg broken cleanly, perfectly apart.

Malus

I look out the window at a seedling crab which has volunteered in the middle of my windflower patch. How to explain my sudden love for this small but uppity thing?

I'm resolved to watch day by day to make certain that it has everything it needs, rain and grief, sunlight and resignation. I couldn't love it more if I had planted it myself.

When you live in a house like mine where every door opens upon an angel standing on his haloed head and his nightie stiff around his legs, a tower of starched muslin, where every pot on the shelf is home to a tiny priest as small as a spider, his stole about his shoulders ready to hear confession, then you'll know that happiness is the contemplation of outdoor growing things their natural order keyed and adamant.

My darling seedling will you flourish? When you're a sapling will you remember who watered you on dry days? And will I still love you when you're four times my height, your boughs full of blossoms and birdsnests? The blossoms fall and the eggs hatch, such a cheeping and squawking to be fed. Thank God when all are fledged and flying. I was almost ready to pay a woodsman to lop everything to the nub.

Leaves obscure the sky as I pray for bitter apples luminous with knowledge, and, when these are fallen, for enough wasps to feed in the splits and brown bruises, enough buzz to drown out the whirr of the holy man's wheel as he chants cross-legged on the grass under the yellowing leaves, while beside him, its dignity not wavering, sits a black dog lustrous and silent as a monk.

*Paradijslaan**

A month's holiday can so easily become a sojourn of years. Stay for awhile and you'll find yourself a citizen of a foreign country, all this in the blink of a farsighted eye. Soon you'll be walking a dog along streets with names in a language which isn't even written in the alphabet you grew up with. Blah. Blah, blah—you're speaking in a twisted tongue you hadn't even heard before you were thirty. You're letting the dog off the leash to run in a park where the grass is a paler green than you ever dreamed of. You're throwing him sticks, you're calling his name, whatever that is. Even your whistling is in a peculiar key you once heard on the radio in a program devoted to oriental music. Is that it? Have you gone East—or South perhaps? Is it natural after all for every bush to blossom with scarlet flowers as big as teacups?

On the way back to your apartment you catch sight of a street you never noticed before. And when you turn down it you are passing plane trees and modest houses built of brick, a substance you haven't seen for years. Aha, you say, I am on my way, and you quicken your walk until it becomes a dance. The dog has left you, of course. You toss away the pointless empty leash.

You are almost there. You are almost home. Number eighteen, number twenty, number twenty-two, the old place. When you knock will anyone open the door? When you press the bell will it echo in the hallway past the hatrack with its five polished brass hooks, past the umbrella stand made from an elephant's forefoot?

It's up to you to decide why you have come back, Aunt says, twisting a grey curl round the second finger of her left hand.

But you know why you've come. Dying is an old-fashioned thing to do and it's best done in the same house where all this began.

No need to hurry. It'll take you a few months you reckon, maybe even a year or two. You will recline on the worn leather sofa. Staring through the window whose wavering glass is like water; you will watch the seasons change the garden. There, pinned to the fence, are the trees you remember as saplings. At times they are bare, at times full of blossom, at times heavy with fruit. And you'll understand at last what Jesus meant when he said to the apostles, *today I have planted three trees for you in Paradise.*

*Paradijslaan is the name of a narrow street in a working class district in Eindhoven, Holland, as I remember it in 1945. The quotation: "Today I have planted three trees for you in Paradise," are words of the Saviour from the Gospel of Thomas.

*Between One Thing and Another**

evening, she says, is very like morning
when the sky is streaked and one pointed star
dangles on a fine string in the window

of understanding   the question
is very clear, but the answer is blurred as though
too many mouths were singing different words
to the same tune

no one can say how many keys
there are to the lock
of music and cutting more
can do no good

let swatches of hair white and gold
fall where they may

and now, she says, I'll lie down
on my bed of prevarications
while the sun apparently gets up, goes down
according to the whim of my lover

you've met him, the one
playing stars and stripes
snakes and ladders
against the twilight sky

obscuring my vision
of angels turning eastward
chanting their creed
affirming their belief in light
and of course in darkness

which after all is nothing
more than the earth mooning
her backside to the sun

**Between one thing and another no time shall intervene.* Julian of Norwich.

Anne Szumigalski
A Statement (1997)

I read in a book: "Is not every child that dies a natural death slain by an Angel?" Aha Mr. Blake, does that explain the sunrise angels sitting on the sill of the East window each finger of their folded hands a fiercely burning flame? Is death by angel something to be desired?

I wander in the woods alone. I sit under a tall pine, the needle duff scratching my eight-year-old bum. The entity that is everything leans down explaining the universe, the oneness, the separateness. I understand how, though we are apart, yet we are one. I understand at once this truth, this whole truth. But by the time I reach home I have forgotten how this works. I can't hold it. It has flown away like a careless bird. Day has ended. The dark night of the soul.

Much later I realize that though we are other from the divine we are sitting in the same chair. This is funny. This is bitter. This is absurd.

Then it is to the absurd, the tragic, the extremely funny I must turn to express that ordinary life beyond logic, beyond time.

And here I am trying to plant that tree once more, trying to build that house again, the one with the angels sitting on the sill of the East window. The sun rises behind their bowed heads. They lean down and write with the fire of their fingers. They may be themselves, they may be myself. I can only copy their words.

Sharon Thesen

SHARON THESEN was born in Tisdale, Saskatchewan, and grew up in western Canadian towns. She attended Simon Fraser University and has been teaching literature and creative writing at Capilano College in North Vancouver since 1976. Six books of her poems have been published, two of which received Governor-General's Award nominations *(Confabulations* and *The Beginning of the Long Dash)*, and four of which were published by the late Coach House Press. She is also the editor of *The New Long Poem Anthology,* also published by Coach House Press. Her poems have appeared in a number of magazines and anthologies, including, most recently, the fourth edition of *20th Century Poetry and Poetics,* edited by Gary Geddes. She currently is editing, with Ralph Maud, a significant correspondence between Charles Olson and Frances Boldereff.

Easter Sunday

ta'wil in *agnosia*
let the light circulate, aerate
the ecstasy

It is my life that is surprised
said Paul Valery
after he had eaten of the fruit

No one sees afterwards.
The light itself circulates
among men and women

given to worship
                                        out of bounds
seeing force in the waves & particles
unbounded

                        see where it ends
the land sinks like a lamp
at daybreak
                            the moth drops to the kitchen table
exhausted

    a sleepy head drops to the pages
drools and dreams so that
                        words stain the mouth

outside   the great tree   tangled
    spaces fill with blue

                                                dream, dream
little sinner, beloved one
nothing
is all you know

The Plenitude

Where would I go
to find you
apart from this side of town
or that, some cafe
or corner of a room
where others are. How carefully
I look at you, moved
& startled, I fuss with my buttons
gesture toward the yellow curtains
gray light window, a talking
for all the world
as if for once it mattered
that the exact description
of the soul not have
a price tag on it,
or that those small gestures
toward the light leave you alone
in your still, half-averted
gaze your gracious wrists

The Stone

Good Friday, fragile
in the mirror, passion
in the music
on the slow radio,
the young mother next door
brings a kitchen chair outside,
lifts her face to the sun.

The first warm day in ages
of rain, cold creeks of it
ran down the windshield
as I drove home, day after day,
over bridges.

It asks to be noticed
that the sun chooses to shine—
or is it that clarity at last
will sear the clouds away
banish confusion, illuminate
the manuscript of our entangled
fingers, relaxed in moonlight—

Those silent rows of monks
come out from solitary
to labour over a complicated beauty—
how did they feel
patiently gilding the garments
& long hair of those two women
who with hands folded or clenched
in grief watch the solemn volunteers
push the stone
across the door
to his body.

The Shroud of Turin

December in Vancouver.
In the mail a small brochure proclaims
the Shroud of Turin, the face of Christ
passport-sized on the cover. The nose
of Christ is long, his beard white,
his eyes closed. Auras and wounds
encircle the crown of his head.

During the day the grass is the unreal green
of moss under streetlights.
The neighbour's birch tree is going bald
from the top down; from its lower branches
dangle a few small orange leaves,
scant survivors of last night's wind.

Poor men from India deliver Christmas
flyers up and down the street.
Dogs bark from behind fences
or from a spot on the sofa
with good visibility between the drapes.
The men don't look up. The bright
flyers are glossy in the sun, they speak
of charge cards and microwaves,
nightgowns and jewels.

In the second-hand clothing store
a spectacular Christmas tree sprouts angels
and candy canes among the worn brown
trousers, old toasters, toe-sculpted shoes.

These objects are from some the source
of a fine lust & are handled with care
by the cashier, who raises her arms
to begin the folding process
of a stained white bedspread, eight dollars.

Rosary

In small rivers
of hours
passing

words grab
as fingers
spread the air

when leaning
down to stretch
interior ligaments

that pull at, hurt
a little
behind the mind—

It feels good
to do this & breathe
coming up

counting pebble
by pebble
my spine

Poem for Norbert's Thesis

Norbert tests the wind recovering
whatever place is for him to see
and say as place, in terms we argue we need
to round the edges of, pat form
into the middle, that form being female
and of stature such as a Queen
enthroned in milky skies of Egypt—
his place to hear songs, words
as bushes and squirrels and small mosses
under the sun in breezes of their own are a choir
of angels. He may dispute "angels" but not
their reality, the long ovals of their dark
open mouths over songbooks the size
of surveyors' maps, their white nighties
and bare feet. Landscape, that troubled
word when it leads to beauty, which
is also a sea, whose metaphors lift
and fall like chromatic scales
in the difficulty of our bodies.

Mythology

With car windows open
on a summer night
the air smells like fish
& an art deco moon
does a balancing act
on the top hat of City Hall—

At the break of night's
yellowing horizon this moon
silverplates someone's destiny, let's say
yours and mine

As if going west
toward those dark blue mountains
made an Egyptian boat
of your worn-out Renault
and we its captive souls
borne along borne along
through the lowing sky

Craning our stiff necks
as we pass the other boatloads
who crane their necks in return,
our shouts

Catapult across the galaxies
& our flashlights are little pinpoints
in the great dark that receives
with open mouth the endless tale
of our lives.

The Broken Cup
(terza rima)

Bits of prosody fall near what remains of me
that drifts on the sofa in a trance
made of loves, lazy rivers, unmended crockery.

I feel so broken now by a too-long dance.
Shot exhausted horses fall behind the stadium
and shards of mirror lance

What could have been a fatal wound, fatal tedium
or a spiritual lesson to have learned
endlessly postponed like closure & delirium.

One wants clear endings, beginnings to burn
big holes through old obdurate patterns, one wants
love to "triumph" as it were but not to earn

A thousand bardos, a daily headache, an ounce
of comfrey for a cure when I am acting up
& slink around ashamed of getting trounced

At life & coping, nearly. Like certain music
refuses transcendence (that strange vulgarity),
and how I threw the broken cup

Away because I know to hope for clarity
where things are broken is just to lie.

After Roy Kiyook's Funeral

I take a kitchen chair out to the front porch
and stand on it to reach the light.
Encased in amber bubbled
glass, which has to be unscrewed
in three small places. The screws are brass,
stiff, unused to suffering. Then the
40 watt bulb comes out and in goes
a 100 watt bulb. The amber casing
back on, with its old cheap bracing
screws. Now
my visitors. Now the path
is lit farther out—and
the way in brighter,
bigger.

Aurora

Garland remains of the starry dynamo surround her

Galactic waterfall shreds & threads over stone

And stone steep downward, the many kilowatts

Feed cities, farms, basement operations.

Get the generator going. Fan blades churn a

Cumulus build-up, lights on, elevator up & down,

Everyone tied to phone or link. The risen cities

Of human splendor, cozy lounge, agencies,

Dog obedience school where two fall in love but there

Are complications not insurmountable, he has tinnitus

She's married eventually they'll join forces

Meantime our Queen beautiful and thrilling

Commanding both pipeline and angels

Evincing wrath at the fleeing night

Aswarm in garlands and little babies, prancing horses

Gilded wheels disperse the dark cumulus the hideous nightmare

The lying awake alone with sore tooth, so beautiful

The beginning of days brightening!

Sharon Thesen
A Bibliography of Spirit

All processionals
Debbie Gibson's deceased aunt's bottle of Chanel No. 5
Richard Grossinger's Planet Medicine: *From Stone-Age Shamanism to Post-Industrial Healing*
Your first forkful of cassoulet in a Toulouse restaurant
Sweet summer breeze off the Assiniboine
The moon in a Chinese poem
The complete works of William Shakespeare
Rhythm
A dog's happiness
English as a second language
All that has been
Vodka martini
A dream in which you are sad that you moved away
Real flowers
Swift path of birds across the skylight
A sunbeam containing physics-particles of your father who has recently passed away
Creeks, streams, and rivers
Colours, especially green, blue, and white, the flag of Earth
Anyone who endures terrible injustice and still loves
An old, old woman called Irene, her careful walking
Finnegans' Wake
Dear little frogs on lilypads
Bird-headed men of ancient Egypt
The cut-outs of Henri Matisse. ("Keep those scissors flashing in the World of Forms, Henri Matisse," in Ed Sander's poem "The Cutting Prow.")
Fantasies of people buying lottery tickets
Bonfire embers
Pretending to be another person, an animal, or a ghost
That which nobody can deny
"A narrow fellow in the grass": E. Dickinson
The Holy Forest
Breath

Miriam Waddington

MIRIAM WADDINGTON was born Dec. 23, 1917 and spent her youth in Winnipeg, Manitoba. Continuing her education in Ottawa, Toronto and Philadelphia, she earned Masters degrees in both Social Work and English Literature, as well as Honourary Doctorates in English from Lakehead and York Universities. Her writing career spans fifty years from the 1945 publication of *Green World,* her first of 13 books of poems, and includes *Collected Poems* from Oxford University Press in 1986. She is also the author of critical volumes on poet A.M. Klein and critic John Sutherland, and the editor of *Jewish Short Stories* (Oxford, 1990), containing her introduction and translations of two Yiddish stories. After a career in social work in Montreal and Toronto, Miriam Waddington joined the faculty of Toronto's York University, where she is now Senior Scholar and Professor Emeritus of English. She has read her poetry and been a guest lecturer at Universities across Canada, and has served as a writer-in-residence at Ottawa University and the Toronto and Windsor Public libraries. Miriam Waddington's poems have been widely translated and have been incorporated in paintings, sculptures and musical compositions by prominent Canadian and U.S. artists and composers. She has twice received the J.I. Segal Prize for the books *Driving Home* (1972) and *Collected Poems* (1986), in addition to the Borestone prize for poetry. Miriam Waddington has lived in Vancouver since 1992.

Traffic Lights at Passover

Here, by some sorcery, lies the avenue
With its boulevard and elms,
Its gracious width of street and stone décor;
A gear flick away, a moment ago
We were on Côte des Neiges with Montreal
Engraved in antique colors on a map below.
The cars like pastel lozenges
Spilled between the bus-bright circuses
And aimed to transcend space
With every moment between nine and five.

If only we could transcend as easily
This dryness which no sense can irrigate
Or travel to, and cross our mountainous griefs
To the legendary valley, there to rest
If not in elms, then firm upon the wings
Of the forgotten angel, death.
Oh seldom-thought-of angel, memory as rare
As Hebrew melodies and rituals once a year
Which speak their melancholy chanting
Through unfamiliar seasonable prayer:

We ate the bitter herbs, but did we pass
Through cleaving oceans? My spirit lay
As dark as Egypt in a solitary kiss,
And the wine held my trembling breath
Upon its surface like a skin;
Grandfather's beaker shone ironically,
And the open door was left
Untranslated for Elijah's coming.

There are no surprises; the light changes,
We shift and fly across the city's desert
To the burgeoning arteries where buildings sway
Above each new oasis; *hayom yom shaini.*
We gulp the gas fumes of the air
And exiled, live another year.
We send our Hebrew God this alien prayer:
Lead us from Egypt and our misplaced faith
To the white paschal lamb and the mayflower
wreath,
And find for us a single leavened hour.

To Be a Healer

All the stubborn unloving husbands are told to me,
and the slothful eighteen-year-old sons
who lie in bed till noon, get slicked up
and go to the pool-room; *(but I thought you knew)*
and the punishing wives and the crooked lovers,
they are all told to me.

What am I to do with all this lumber,
this love-lack, this tear-sacked mother
who argues with the angel of death in a back room?
Or the stepdaughter, dumb as an animal,
she has long ago been screamed off-center,
or even the old drunkard, spirited to the end,
(would it be asking too much, miss,
if I gave you a little kiss?)

And worse, the wasted fountains that rage
against children and neighbours and people
on the public transportation system; the world
is so innocent, and *(you don't know what it is*
to love a boy, but you've heard of it, I'll bet);
he promises to get a job and stay sober.

All this spits and sprays me,
and I have to remind myself to stand against it
and I have to remind myself there was once
another well
just as bottomless in which I drowned
not in anger or in hate; that well was deep too,
its water was sweeter than light and more
faithful,
and steadfast all my life long.

Fortunes

There is something in all of us
pure and unconsumable;
after the forest fires
on the logged-over hillsides
you find the stubborn flowering
of fireweed or a green tree
hung with a grab-bag of prophecies:
you will live long you will go on ocean voyages
you will be lucky in love or unlucky
beware the queen of spades a handsome stranger
will come into your life the choices
are dazzling.

But whatever you do
it will end the same;
we are not all lucky and the stranger came
but stayed a stranger   we lived
unhappily ever after and the queen of spades
dug my grave; after the ten thousandth evening
of dumb show and furious pantomime
fed up with Punch and Judy
I went out into the autumn night
to cry my anger to the stone-blind fields
just as I was, untraditional, North American,

Jewish, Russian, and rootless in all four,
religious, unaffiliated, and held
in a larger-than-life seize of hate.

It was then I felt my own purity:
I felt the young girl in me
still like a green tree growing,
tall and rooted, with a promise of flowering,
whatever bastardy flower I could flower with now.
a *shloime-kapoir* Solomon-upside-down flower;
and why not? I always think of the Russian word
for soul, *dusha,* and the dusty Slavic village
smelling so sweet with the grass uncut
and the white lilacs blooming, like a homecoming
for my homeless half-and-half soul.

And I felt a kind of raised eyebrow
yes-this-is-me   this is no one else,
not the laidly worm of Spindlestone,
no longer the bewitched princess
but a wonderful living statue of marble stone
with her garments sculptured,
sailing against the wind of death.

The Field of Night

for Philip Surrey

Messiah will not come
and I must sing the time
that every poet knows
so ravel up the threads
the golden fleece of song,
seize armfuls of cloud
above the gilded domes
of Moscow's onion roofs
and spin the world around.

And I will read the time
from sundials in the air
where London used to sleep
and Paris frivolous
danced on teetering feet;
the hives of all New York
swarmed in the trees
and neighbours did not keep
to caves and private work.

Our cowardice is known
and all the ill is done,
alone or with another
the body is our brother
and Messiah will not come
though we may wait the time
till kings of good become
the presidents of wrong;
there's nothing left but time.

Such time as others shape
to their elected hopes
with songs that rise above
the golden concert halls
or reach of telescopes;
there my defeated choirs
sing in broken keys
of all the doors I forced
with solar acts of love.

The wind has howled them shut
and sealed them in my blood;
and all the frozen songs
that winter in the north
lie on a field of night,
they wait the touch of sun
and I am sick and dumb;
the fastness of the world!
Messiah when will you come?

A Man is Walking

A man is walking toward me
with leaning green rhythms
the sky falls away   shoulders
him like a green hood.

The man looks familiar:
as he comes closer   I see
that it is my father and
he is bringing me flowers

Not ordinary flowers—
but a whole tree of them
torn up by the roots
dripping with the blood

Of earth with the earth
of his grave in the green
graveyard; and on this day
he arose to bring me flowers,

And I am startled   imagine him
bringing me flowers and speaking
my name with the old melancholy
shaking his head and saying:

your poems daughter are dark
very dark, there is too much
darkness in the world, go and
plant these broken roots

in the garden and hurry now
they are lythrum   fireweed,
remember how you saw them
growing wild every summer

on the way to Gimli   hurry
now and plant them   we have such
drying winds on the prairies such
drying winds in the graveyard.

My father is walking towards
me with green rhythms my
father is bringing me flowers
to plant and he is saying

Just as he used to say   *there*
will be no more cruelty
no more death no more dark
words: for you there will be

Only rivers rivers   the
timeless green of rivers
moving and singing their
fertile song to your years.

A Morning Like the Morning When Amos Awoke

Let me sing
of reality
let me forget
the contingencies—
houses mortgages
cars children
music lessons
loneliness;
let me sing
of the terrible
cities the dry
furnaces when
autumn was
spread over

Manhattan and
brandy burned
in the (polluted)
air and Hart
Crane's Indian
maiden danced
on the autumn
water of the
icy Hudson:

Whitman's lilacs
were folded deep
in his leaves of
grass loose manu-
scripts planted
with people (and
this was almost
the last week to
be wearing sandals)
and all the time
the crabapples were
ripening behind
my back in a
Toronto garden
just like on the
morning when Amos
awoke from his
figsticking job
on his father's
estate and filled
the world with
his stern *take*
away from me the
noise of your songs
to the melody of
your harps I will
not listen but
let justice roll
down like waters.

Let me sing of
reality forget
the contingencies
to the melody of
harps I will not
listen   take away
from me the noise
of my songs.

Elijah

Elijah's gone to Poland
as naked as William Blake,
his beard is as black as a chimney,
his eyes are a Baltic lake.

He sifts the mounds of rubble,
broken bottles and lead,
Elijah counts his children,
his Warsaw children are dead.

The Jewish *seder* is over
and Jerusalem's song is still,
Poland spills with echoes
but Elijah's beaker is full

Of night as black as the chimneys
and the wailing of William Blake,
Elijah sits in Poland
and sips his own heartbreak.

What the Angel Said

Caedmon dreamed
that an angel
came to him and
said: *sing* and
he awoke and sang.

I dreamed that
a man in a white
shirt sewn with
stars rose out
of the scrolls

of the snowy sea
and the angel
turned to me and
said: love and I
awoke and loved.

How Old Women Should Live

Old women
should live like worms
under the earth,
they should come out
only after a good rain.

Or be the kind of worm
that lives in flour
that has stood too long
and when discovered
is thrown away in disgust
by the good housewife.

Or be a wood-worm
that patiently winds
its journey through
history's finest
furniture like those
old women we see
in the corridors of
nursing homes.

Or they should be
constructive like the
silk-worm who lives
on nothing but a box
of mulberry leaves in
hot China too far away
to bother anyone.

The wisest old women
imitate the glow-worm
who is never seen by day
with all its grey worminess
and shrivelled feet,
but shines wise and warm
only after dark.

Old women should be
magical like those worms
in transition and chrysalis
from egg to butterfly;
even decrepit old women
can turn into butterflies
in the third existence
promised to us all.

MIRIAM WADDINGTON

And remember that worms
are fussy about where
they live and what they eat;
they like warmth, darkness,
and good nourishment and
sometimes when it suits them
they like to come out in
all their loose nakedness
to crawl in the sun.

The Angels Who Sweep II

1
The silence of angels:
their words are hushed
in the murmur of snow,
when they look up
from their sweeping
their brooms are frozen,
caught in the stillness
of winter's mid-air.

They incline their heads
they are listening
to Beethoven play
his bursting song
when prisoners first see
the blinding light
through their barred
and buried windows.

2
The red lanterns of angels
hang waiting in mid-air
and the bells
in the golden throats
of church spires
ring between silences.

3
The blessed silence
of angels; like those
Sunday morning silences
when we walked through
city streets that were
half-asleep and empty,
and only the smells
of fresh bread and coffee
drifted down with us
to the river.

4
And the streets
in those days stretched
across shining bridges
to the unknown prairie
and the ripening future;
unmindful
we walked on the bridges
and admired the lacy
fretwork crocheted from
silvery steel by some
giant hand.

5
We did not ask
whose was the hand
we did not read
the specific gravity
of girders or guess
at the composition,
the depth of the pilings.

6
Locked in our separate
trances we joined
the invisible procession
towards what was still
undisclosed; and the angels
with the red lanterns
hovered over us,
their wings brushed us
with silence and the silence
was the silence
of the angels who sweep.

7
In our hearts we knew
it was not really summer.

An Interview with Miriam Waddington (December 1996, Vancouver, B.C.)

SM: Jewish rituals and traditions figure in many of your poems, such as "Traffic Lights at Passover." Is there a longing in your work for some connection with authentic ritual or spiritual practice?

MW: I'm afraid not. I don't connect through rituals. Maybe it's because I grew up in a family that didn't practice them. Yet I think there's a difference between traditions and rituals. I like traditions, but rituals are something else. Rituals, unless they have some inner meaning for the person who's practising them, are really very phoney; 90% of what I read and hear is not authentic.

SM: Maybe you could speak more about your sense of tradition.

MW: Well, tradition is a sense of continuity more than anything, and there certainly are very definite traditions in Jewish literature and history. I know Yiddish literature and three great turn-of-the-century writers—Sholom Aleichem, Mendele Mocher Sforim, and Y.L. Peretz—as well as other writers who wrote in America. They combined traditions of religion with contemporary issues. Our rituals don't always contain those connections, but a good writer can make them. There isn't much spirituality in contemporary life because everything is all about money.

SM: Some Jewish writers have remained true to their cultural heritage. Leonard Cohen, for instance, though a secular writer in many ways, and a student of Zen Buddhism, acknowledges the centrality of his Jewish heritage. At one point in an interview he argued for the value of exploring one's own tradition rather than going further afield.

MW: Yes, of course. However, most of us have been brought up in a Christian society. Certainly we absorb elements of Christianity. In my time, at least, we were educated in Christian schools, and by teachers who were Christians. So I'm sure that a lot of Christianity rubs off on us. I remember telling my friend Adele Wiseman, "When I was in Jerusalem, I walked the stations of the cross, and you know, Adele, I felt very sorry for Jesus as I wandered those stations. I identified with him, and thought it must have been terrible to be dragged through those streets." She said, "What's wrong with you, Miriam? You must have been depressed." She was shocked that I should even think that way.

SM: Yet hasn't there always been a great deal of intermingling between Christianity and Judaism down through the centuries?

MW: Of course. Christianity started as a branch of Judaism. It's interesting, there has always been anti-Semitism in the world too. There's a Jewish writer called Aharon Applefeld. He lives in Israel and writes in Hebrew, and his books are wonderful. He has explored the question of why the Jews are hated. He comes to the conclusion it's because of Christianity, but he never says so explicitly.

SM: I just finished reading *The Origin of Satan* by Elaine Pagels, a scholar of early Christianity, and she argues that books like the Gospel of John have been used throughout western history to perpetrate anti-Semitism or to demonize whoever the "other" happens to be at the time. The medieval church, for instance, blamed the Jews for the death of Jesus, and the Jews have always been associated with evil, the "other." Then the Church began attacking its heretics, like the Cathars.

MW: Oh sure, and what were the Crusades all about?

SM: Some people try to make a distinction between the institution and the inner essence of a religion, which might imply a distinction, for instance, between Jesus and what the Church made of him later.

MW: I know that Jesus did not teach hatred of the Jews. After all, he was one. But when I studied Anglo Saxon we would read the homilies by various writers from that period, and they all ended up saying that the Jews are going to suffer in the life after death because they crucified Christ.

SM: So, how does this concern with anti-Semitism reflect itself in your work?

MW: I felt it keenly as a child growing up in Canada. It was rampant. For instance, before the war you couldn't teach or even get a job as a chambermaid in a hotel if you were a Jew or had a Jewish name. Nowadays, names can be as outlandish as you like. Maybe the more outlandish the better. And I think that's a good development, but it wasn't so before the war. It was terrible. The kids on the block would call you "dirty Jew." You got it everywhere you went. It seems to me present today in a lesser way, except it's not condoned by society.

SM: In your poem "Fortunes," the speaker describes herself as "untraditional, North American/Jewish, Russian, and rootless in all four,/ religious, unaffiliated." Do you still feel rootless, though you have lived in Canada all your life?

MW: Yes, the Canadian landscape is my landscape and I feel less rootless here than I do anywhere else. I feel connected to the Canadian landscape, the Prairie landscape particularly. But as far as the sense of exile goes, I feel that if you're a Jew and you're an artist, you're always going to be an exile. I think every artist feels as though he or she is exiled.

SM: The poem "To a Healer" seems to come out of your experience as a social worker. To what extent is poetry for you an act of healing or regeneration for the writer, the reader, even society? How does it address issues of social justice?

MW: I think anything creative is healing, because what happens when you make something, write something, paint something is...(well, you know the old Platonic notion that the self is separated into the mental and the emotional?) What happens in art is that they're unified. So since to be unified is to feel good, that is healing, if you like. That's what art does, it gives you a sense of wholeness.

SM: Is that sense of wholeness connected to some sense of "holiness" or the divine for you?

MW: Well, I never think about it as divine. I feel that it's a great privilege to be able to write or paint or do something creative, and that, in a sense, artists have a big responsibility. I've never thought much about responsibility, but I'm sure it is there, because art doesn't come just from the self. I don't want to call it spiritual, but it's not really the individual only. And it isn't something that the individual is totally responsible for.

SM: So is there a sense of something larger moving through you?

MW: That's right. And you're lucky if it has touched you, but it's not anything you can will into existence.

SM: My next question has to do with your interest in the Hebrew prophets and your use of them in your work, figures like Amos, Elijah, and your namesake Miriam, for instance.

MW: Well, first of all I went to a Yiddish parochial day school for the first five years of my life and learned a lot of Jewish history. Then later, in some of the higher grades, we studied the Tanach, the Old Testament in Yiddish translation. The prophet Amos is very sympathetic because he was the first to write down his prophecies. Before that they were just spoken. His story is interesting. He worked on his father's fig ranch; he was an agricultural worker. Then he had these marvellous dreams. When he had these dreams he felt he should go into the city and preach, because they were dreams of destruction of the people, fires and so on. They were good metaphors. One was a basket of fruit, one was a wall of fire. So he goes into the city, into Jerusalem, which was run by the priests, who were pretty commercial. The Temple was very commercial. They sold a lot of merchandise, made money from selling doves for sacrifice and so on. Amos preached outside the Temple against war, against oppressing the poor, against charging interest. The priests were annoyed and went to the king and complained, "This man claims he's a prophet; he's out there in front of the Temple, preaching against war and against commerce, so we want him killed." So the king said, "Well, he says he's a prophet. Maybe he is. So we won't kill him. We'll just banish him to his family farm." So that's what they did. They banished him. But he is the prophet of justice who wrote: "Let justice rain down like waters." I call him the patron saint of writers because he was the first to write down his prophecies.

SM: Do you think there's a strong connection between poetry and prophecy in your work?

MW: I wouldn't have the *chutzpah* to call myself a prophet. I think it's enough to call myself a writer.

SM: But isn't there a side of your work that calls for social justice and uses poetry to do it?

MW: Yes, but it's subtle. I do have a poem called "Polemics" against war, and a poem called "The Milk of the Mothers" against nuclear destruction. I have many poems against war. And my poem "The Women's Jail" is against poverty for women.

SM: When you start to think about it, there's quite an accumulation of material on these sorts of themes. Finally, I'd like to ask about "The Angels Who Sweep" poems, where angels seem to be associated with silence and mystery. Can you elaborate on what they represent in your work?

MW: Mystery, I think, mystery. I don't really know where that image came from, but it did come long before people were writing about angels.

SM: Yes, it's something of a fad now. Chubby puttis dancing on ceilings.

MW: Oh, it is a fad. But these weren't that kind of angel. I have this image of men sweeping the street car tracks in Winnipeg from when I was growing up. Their red lanterns were swinging. They had to come and sweep to get the snow off the tracks. So I imagine that is where it probably originated. They became angels who sweep. The image came into my head. It was given. I didn't analyze it. You don't know where these things come from or stop to bother. These images are in the air. And I believe that artists articulate them. But they're not entirely from inside of the person. They are collective.

SM: Are you saying, then, that there is some quality of "otherness" in the poetic process?

MW: Yes, but it isn't just an aspect of your own psyche. I believe those images are in the atmosphere and that artists are more sensitive at feeling them. They speak to some people and not to others.

David Zieroth

DAVID ZIEROTH has reclaimed his original first name. As Dale, he published four books of poetry: *Clearing: Poems from a Journey* (Anansi, 1973), *Mid-River* (Anansi, 1981), *When the Stones Fly Up* (Anansi, 1985) and *The Weight of My Raggedy Skin* (Polestar, 1991). *How I Joined Humanity at Last* (Harbour, 1998) is his most recent book. He teaches creative writing at Douglas College in New Westminster, B.C. where he edited *Event: The Douglas College Review* from 1985 to 1996. His poetry has appeared in *Reconcilable Differences: The Changing Face of Poetry by Canadian Men since 1970*, an anthology edited by Christopher Levenson (Bayeux, 1994), and *Poetry: An Introduction*, edited by Michael Meyer (Bedford Books, 1995). He is included in *The Oxford Companion to Twentieth-Century Poetry in English* (1994) and in *The Oxford Companion to Canadian Literature* (1997). He lives in North Vancouver, B.C. He has two daughters.

This Side

It's hard to listen all the time:
the voice of who you are
coming at you.

Sometimes you hear another voice,
as if from behind a green hedge
where I might be walking

where poems slip out of my head
hit the ground and start blooming.

On this side of the light
I listen as hard as I can.

Function of the Individual

The function of the individual
he realizes as he travels through town
is to provide the lightning strike
to matter.
What God once did in beautiful
biblical illustrations
he now must do.
The waterfront, for instance,
must be charged up, revved higher
until, incandescent, it shimmers and soothes
the men and women
who stumble mornings
out of the Seabus
and into time.

Loathsome are some of those bodies.
But he sees them now
as uncharged lumps
unable to grip
the time they have in this
configuration of weary mouth and heavy plunging step.
Up the escalator he rides with them,
careful not to step in front
of those who wander
with their demons.
The cruise ship out the window
has arrived at dawn
and now from its white sides
happy angels watch and watch
and are ignored in turn.

All travellers move time
aside as they go, and as they pass by
it changes, collects, leaps ahead again
so each travels through
what has been shucked off
and waits patiently
for the lightning eye to burn it up
to the cloudy thin-cloudy sky seen in the sea,
in the harbour's oil and white wave.

Thinking My Neighbour's Thoughts

One day I stepped out
of my apartment and walked
down the hall to the entrance,
and passed another door not unlike
my own; it, too, had a spy hole
through which I could have seen nothing
had I ventured to look in;

its numbers although different
from my own were yet near enough
to be almost mine.
As I passed by
I heard the noise, unmistakable
in its holding back and wrenching out,
of sobbing, and I froze there
and imagined the head tipped back,
the hands covering the face,
the mouth twisted—
and then I went on my way.

I have never seen
in these many months
the face behind that door,
I have never seen
who authored that anguish
on the day I was free to pass
and go outside into the unexpected
blue daylight of a winter sky.
Part of me simply went on,
stepping out to catch the air
on my cheeks and lips,
testing the whiteness of the street
with my soles to see
if I might slide
in my greeting of the day.

And part of me watched
everything I did, each step and sniff,
each thought of step and sniff,
and this part remembered
back to the room and door
behind which another watcher
crumpled on the couch.
This part scouted ahead
of the sun and breeze
and knew where I would pass
later in the day, near to evening,

and the question would be
not whether I would knock or pry
but rather how to say
(to him or her who lived within)
that beyond the thing wrung out of us
and the thought of the thing
and the observation of the thing,
frost has melted on the street,
and a great circle of flame
has been close at hand all day.

Once Again Among the Humans

It is so simple a need: to feel
God stirring once again among the humans,
in the cleverness, the capacities,
along the eyebrows and out through the prickle
of the skin—to be drenched
in God as you are sometimes
caught in a downpour and find yourself
not running for the old doorway
but stopping to be washed,
the umbrella down on the ground and the cold
dividing the hair on your head.

Flesh itself can take you
places, but you return to gnaw
on broken, unreleased, unreleasable matter,
the gloom you always feel
when you only want to feel
something more than your own machine.
Where else can you look? We've given up
flowers, our lovers' bodies, the descant
of the monk's chant: these sweet connectors
thrilled in the blood and mind

but what you seek is
not a murmur or a word,
not a vowel, not a breath
entering or shuddering out, nothing less
than union
beyond pain, weariness, sex, irony,
beyond mystery to inertia of the sort
a child will use to imagine
angels are watching and from time to time
interfering, causing cars to veer away from
a precious pet now out prowling
among the darkening, gold-flecked streets
you suddenly find yourself hurrying along
watching for an entrance.

On the Path of Inner Development

There would have to be trees,
and in the trees, birds, but
first the trees: great cages of light
which shake down
some peace in those moments
I stray away from the needs
of the animals and the children
to lean like a schoolboy
and gaze nowhere but up
through a river of light, triggering
on that leaf, the way it signals
and routes sun out of heaven and straight
onto the back of my hand
before I am snatched away by a greater
blast of light, this one opening
past the big branch just above me
and going up so high I shift away
for fear I might fall off the ground
and into the air and turn and turn

and vanish and touch the last green thing
with my outstretched hand and find myself
going into the sound of my own A-a-ah—

The birds' giddy witnessing
I see first in my usual way.
As little ones, sparrows or finches,
they hurry each other
in among the leaves, and this
hustle draws me out of myself
and I discover my surprise
in their flashes of colour, the sharpness
of the eye in the one who hovers down close,
the sparkle of the beak,
the power of the crest—and I remember
out of nowhere the night bird
who comes so often to me of late, crying
just as I turn to sleep
its call of two notes
so like my own name, until I feel
my body wants to move, throw back the covers
and run to the window and see.

But now, here, under the tree
wings return to their grey shapes
and I stand up into mine
so the blood slides into action
and I continue making my way
out from under delight into the sun
until wind blurs that point
on the horizon I once thought
I had to reach but which now seems no more
than someone's idea of the place to begin.

The Poplars of St. Vital
for Walter and Tashi

These trees catch at winds
flung out of sky and sun
in gusts aimed to be elsewhere;
they define the street
by bowing down to the park.
And I bend, too, and see
my shoes need replacing soon,
which means: going to the stores
with the money required
for leather uppers;
which means: where leather
originates—and the factory!—
for relief, I return to my friend
who has somehow untangled himself
from the race without denying
any of us—
which leads to talk.
The dog returns with wetness from the river
and flings it happily about
and we raise our hands to ward off
the worst of it, not wanting
his little joke;
he is already composing
intelligent dog-thoughts
about this trip, the pleasant
weariness that will flop him down,
the old shoe he tossed once and
left, the other dogs he spoke to
in appropriate ways so they would know
his master and his friend
were not to be dallied with,
the sense of the circle he made
once again, how sufficient it felt,
especially the paths through the poplars
many others have taken.

So we follow the happy dog
and I unburden myself without
dumping; we smell the river
and are grateful although
its raw red line
can reek of sewage, more risk
in this long life on a small planet
judged to be scientifically alone
even as our hi-tech runners
scuff along the bank
and our inner chemistry
strains hugely for
some cosmological love
untouched by how we change.

Question

1.

Is my soul a cup of milk
that once taken

spreads into every capillary
giving me a personality

to fit Friday
or Monday with all its moods?

2.

When I was afraid to say
I had a soul, did I imagine

I would leave it in a cafeteria line,
with the half-eaten muffin

for some white-clad worker
to carry off?

When I was young enough to believe
reason, why didn't reason

bear me up the stairs
of my father's house

to sleep the sleep of peace,
happy logic in my head?

3.

When this soul came to me
what animal peace

fell from me, and when I fell in love
how did my soul know

that here was chemistry
come round again to try

joining another
it could never finally touch?

4.

Can't electrons alone
animate my hand

so it can place and put,
stroke or strike?

A man comes to a woman
and the cells divide—could you fix

a more strange plan?
Or imagine

the entry of the soul
at some disputable moment

and without fanfare
in bedrooms, guest

houses everywhere? The non-thing
among hips and moans?

5.

What if I slip one night
into a dream and bang my head

so hard I leave my body behind?
Is my soul this dream of light

returning to itself?
Is it time

carried in a pocket
and going farther away?

6.

When my soul leaves me
will it fly like an owl

to the nearest height of land
to watch,

its golden eyes
solemn but without grief?

Body floating,
apparently set to drift,

I look into your eyes,
—and why can't I see you

before you came here
by saying

mother, father,
birthmark, skin?

7.

My own soul,
did it grow out of childhood

or was it bestowed?
Has it always been?

My old dog when I was young,
did he know?

Did my mother?
Did everyone

have some part lighter
than bone, longer than blood?

Three Trees

The three trees outside my window
have their different views of what I do
but each morning they dote
on the sun, their nearly
identical apical meristems
straining to the light;
afternoons they bend more
toward one another as if
commenting on the deciduous mass
that clutters the ravine,
on sad signs of decay
now the bark beetle has brought brown
to stay. Then
the wind picks up and the three
take to humming, setting off a sound
as old as ice
and without the drumming trouble
of the far-off cottonwoods.
By night they change, I swear,
and look my way
to see what's been denied
to seedlings
intended only to grow just so,
given to one plot,
starting and stopping in this spot.
The large one watches
and comes to know by night
the movements of my to and fro;
I stand sometimes and look beyond
her bulk, then hurry on to eat
and shake and bend—and then
grow still
when the green wind comes in
the dark window. I end up always
in bed where the other two
with a tilt of my head

come into view, and all night they
watch over me, in kinship with
my rootedness in sheets,
my only movements slight
or not at all: the flinging out of arms
and dreams of arms
no different from the sway
when birds alight,
big ones to scan
for food, the smaller hearts
gripping hard as they sing.

The Gulf of Heaven

Between what we need to know
and what we come to believe
lies the Gulf of Heaven
we cross daily
swimming to that farther shore
which bears its joyful name
because only there are we free
from the uncertainty
after the last bit of love
lets us down for the day
and we have to call on
the reserves
to arise.

Once I thought
I could push across
by myself: I was young,
I had my father's voice
to make me think
I was a big tough lad.
But blood bubbles
into ideas, and not one

helped me swim the expanse
after zoology class,
in the cold, on Furby Street,
imagination and Sherry Denbo
pushing against me
as if they were
answers.
                                        Now I move from
what I hope is truly true
to what I discover
I believe. And I have begun to believe
in the breast stroke and the butterfly stroke
because of their beautiful names
and because I believe heaven must be
perfectly conjured and framed,
each wave falling back
beside my head to show me
glowing green land
and the hot shore.

The Mouse and My Mother

The mouse in the house
reminds me my mother now
long dead fled
her black hair flying from snakes
who themselves chased mice
for food so they could continue
to chase. The mouse here
caught in a live trap
is taken outside, its head
large on its body, its eye
large in its head, safe
now to find other houses
and begin its tiny noises in the night

—or perhaps return to us
as I feel some days my mother
returns to me: after weeks
when I haven't considered her
suddenly I feel her close
not scrabbling in the walls
or dashing past my foot but gentler
in her announcement, a rocking
at the base of thought, a nosy
poking friendliness as if she
happened to be passing by and felt
the need to drift my way
for surely if she *is*
then how big a place she must be in,
big as the house is big
to that little one who finds us
sleeping and cuts along the walls
in search of crumbs
or the soft material out of which
a nest is built and filled
and more and more is pulled
out of nothing into form.

David Zieroth
Spirit and Poetry

This past summer I went to see a psychic for the first time. Wilhelmina said she would see pictures over my right shoulder. With her German accent and sparky, open face, she reminded me a little of my mother, and I felt immediately at ease. During the half-hour session that followed I found myself laughing more than once, so candid and clear were her pictures. When I arrived at her door, she knew nothing about me, not even my name, and yet she scored hit after hit about my occupation, my personality, my worries, and—who knows?—my future.

I left her feeling reassured about my children and my path, among other anxieties. But what was thrilling was the nature of our encounter: she had been able to open herself so completely she could then access something of me. I began to think of her as a performance artist.

Did she take the stuff that emanated from me—my highest hopes, my deepest dreads—and turn them into pictures? She saw me climbing an ever-narrowing wall until at the very top I had no place to stand. I had to choose between falling back the way I had come or jumping forward. (I jumped, which she assured me was the better choice.) She spoke in metaphors, turning the outpourings of my spirit into images she fed back to me, telling me who I was. It seems to me poetry does much the same work, of witnessing, translating, imaging, relaying.

Now psychics are not necessarily spiritual. When we talk about spiritual matters, we are concerned with some larger vision beyond the hits and misses of our own self-centredness. Nevertheless, my experience with Wilhelmina pushed me to think about the unchallenged assumptions I had lived with for so long they had begun to evolve into a belief system. She had seen me closing a large church door, and she said I would not open it again. That observation seemed right to me. I had fought my way out of a sometimes narrow Protestant upbringing into the light of a young man's reason. But I had not turned my back on the life of the spirit. Writing and reading poetry for over thirty years had attuned me to the large and little movements of my soul.

And so I now had a chance to articulate and affirm the beliefs that had grown up in me. First, I was more and more convinced that only reincarnation could explain the strangeness and particularity of our vicissitudes; it felt right, something stolen away from reason and surrendered to. Second, I could imagine a consciousness that predates the physical universe. On some days these beliefs coincide to make me feel as though I am a requirement of the universe without my knowing why, and a surprising sense of poise develops as a result. Then openness prevails, helping to counter the angst and fear that surge up periodically with great force. Views like these have gained ground in me, almost without my noticing, and have replaced the concept of a random universe; more importantly, through them I can begin to move beyond my accustomed, contemporary mode of irony and suffering.

To move thus in my life is to move likewise in my poetry. My poetry is not at the centre of my life; I am. When I focus too much on poetry, it fades away, can't live under the glare. But when I turn to my life, looking always to be conscious of the quality of its spirit, then the poetry lives on its own from ground out of which it can rise naturally. Intention, I've come to realize, is one of the connections to spirit. It's my intention to give poetry the power to grasp the faces of my spirit I cannot express in any other way.

To keep my spirit up: that's the task, and the tools at hand include solitude, mountains, walks by water, peppermint tea, conversations with friends on porches and in parks, and of course poetry. Poetry revives the spirit, acknowledges its presence and importance, softens the cynicism that threatens it, draws us away from our desperate dance with materialism. But where do poems come from? How do these pictures come to me? How does Wilhelmina know what she knows? The questions are off the mark. She works in much the same way I work as a poet: moving by image and intuition, the idea made manifest, the spirit made word. When I am most open, most conscious, I am most me, a spirit most happy as a poem.

November, 1996

ACKNOWLEDGEMENTS

ELIZABETH BREWSTER: "For the unknown goddess" from *Selected Poems of Elizabeth Brewster: 1944-1977* by Elizabeth Brewster reprinted by permission of Elizabeth Brewster and Oberon Press, Copyright Elizabeth Brewster 1985. "Creation," "Dinah and Her Brethren" and "Tamar's Story" from *Garden of Sculpture* by Elizabeth Brewster reprinted by permission of Elizabeth Brewster and Oberon Press, Copyright Elizabeth Brewster, 1998. "Creation" appeared previously in *Prairie Fire.* Selections from "Footnotes to the Book of Job" from *Footnotes to the Book of Job* reprinted by permission of Elizabeth Brewster and Oberon Press, Copyright Elizabeth Brewster 1995. Interview with Elizabeth Brewster conducted in Victoria, B.C., March 1997, printed by permission of author, Copyright Elizabeth Brewster 1997.

ROBERT BRINGHURST: All poems in this anthology from *The Calling: Selected Poems 1970-1995* by Robert Bringhurst reprinted by permission of Robert Bringhurst and McClelland & Stewart Inc. The Canadian Publishers, Toronto, Copyright Robert Bringhurst 1995. Prose piece "In Praise of Vacant Lots" by Robert Bringhurst published by permission of author, Copyright Robert Bringhurst 1997.

LEONARD COHEN: All poems in this anthology from *Stranger Music: Selected Poems and Songs* by Leonard Cohen reprinted by permission of Leonard Cohen Stranger Music, Inc. and McClelland & Stewart Inc. The Canadian Publishers, Toronto, Copyright Leonard Cohen and Leonard Cohen Stranger Music, Inc. 1993. "Anthem" by Leonard Cohen, c. 1993 Sony/ATV Songs LLC; "If It Be Your Will," by Leonard Cohen, c. 1985 Sony/ATV Songs LLC. All rights for both songs administered by Sony/ATV Music Publishing, 8 Music Sq. West, Nashville, TN 37203.

LORNA CROZIER: "Myths" from *The Garden Going On Without Us* by Lorna Crozier reprinted by permission of Lorna Crozier and McClelland & Steward Inc., The Canadian Publishers, Toronto, Copyright Lorna Crozier 1985. "Angel of Infinity" from *Angels of Flesh, Angels of Silence* by Lorna Crozier reprinted by permission of Lorna Crozier and McClelland & Stewart Inc. The Canadian Publishers, Toronto, Copyright Lorna Crozier 1988. "On the Seventh Day," "Inventing the Hawk," and "The Language of Angels" from *Inventing the Hawk* by Lorna Crozier reprinted by permission of Lorna Crozier and McClelland & Stewart Inc. The Canadian Publishers, Toronto, Copyright Lorna Crozier 1992. "Naming the Light," "The Souls of Animals," and "Noah's Wife" from *Everything Arrives at the Light* by Lorna Crozier reprinted by permission of Lorna Crozier and McClelland &

Stewart Inc. The Canadian Publishers, Toronto, Copyright Lorna Crozier 1995. "Country Dweller" and "Wilderness" from *A Saving Grace: The Collected Poems of Mrs. Bentley* by Lorna Crozier reprinted by permission of McClelland & Stewart Inc. The Canadian Publishers, Toronto, Copyright Lorna Crozier 1996. Prose piece by Lorna Crozier, "Two Goldfish in the Snow," printed by permission of Lorna Crozier, Copyright Lorna Crozier 1996.

Barry Dempster: "Souls," "Angels and Poems" and "In Search of Mary" from *Positions to Pray In* by Barry Dempster reprinted by permission of Barry Dempster and Guernica Editions, Copyright Guernica Editions and Barry Dempster 1989. "Adam and Innocence" from *The Unavoidable Man* by Barry Dempster reprinted by permission of Barry Dempster and Quarry Press, Copyright Barry Dempster 1990. "Hampstead 1915" and "A Million Words....Vence 1930" from *Letters from a Long Illness with the World: the D.H. Lawrence Poems* by Barry Dempster reprinted by permission of Barry Dempster and Brick Books, Copyright Barry Dempster 1993. "Sunday School and the Promised Land," "Three Prayers," "Holy Face" and "Octaves" from *Fire and Brimstone* by Barry Dempster reprinted by permission of Barry Dempster and Empyreal Press, Copyright Barry Dempster 1997. Prose piece by Barry Dempster printed by permission of author, Copyright Barry Dempster 1996.

Sky Dancer Louise B. Halfe: "Ghost Dance," "Spirits," "Pāhkahkos", "Nōhkom ātayohkān," and "Elder's Waltz" from *Bear Bones and Feathers* by Louise Halfe reprinted by permission of Louise B. Halfe and Coteau Books, Copyright Louise B. Halfe 1996 (Third Printing). "Spirits" and "Pāhkahkos" first appeared in *Writing the Circle: Native Women of Western Canada* (*NeWest Review*). "Possession took me last night," "Pē-nihtacowēk," and "Ram Woman" from *Blue Marrow* by Skydancer Louise B. Halfe reprinted by permission of Louise B. Halfe and McClelland & Stewart Inc. The Canadian Publishers, Toronto, Copyright Louise B. Halfe 1997. "The Tears that Wove our Songs" by Skydancer Louise B. Halfe reprinted by permission of Louise B. Halfe, appeared in an earlier form in *NeWest Review* (April/May 1995). This piece was also published in the *Click Anthology* (Fall 1997) by Macfarlane Walter & Ross, and in *Blue Marrow*, reprinted by permission of Louise B. Halfe and McClelland & Steward, Copyright Louise B. Halfe 1998.

Dennis Lee: "The Gods," "Nightwatch (Back with the scotch)," "Cadence," "Hunger," and "Heart Residence" from *Nightwatch: New & Selected Poems 1968-1996* by Dennis Lee reprinted by permission of Dennis Lee and McClelland & Stewart Inc. The Canadian Publishers, Toronto, Copyright Dennis Lee 1996. "The Gods" appeared in 1978 as a Kanchenjunga Press chapbook and was reprinted in *The Gods* (McClelland & Stewart 1979). Excerpts from the essay, "Poetry and

Unknowing," by Dennis Lee originally published in *Poetry and Knowing: Speculative Essays & Interviews*, edited by Tim Lilburn, reprinted by permission of Dennis Lee and Quarry Press, Copyright for the authors 1995; based on an interview conducted by Michael Higgins, Peter Hinchcliffe, and John Porter which appeared in *The New Quarterly*, Summer 1994.

TIM LILBURN: "Hosanna to Wisdom, the Divine Anima" and "Theophany and Argument" from *Names of God* by Tim Lilburn reprinted by permission of Tim Lilburn and Oolichan Books, Lantzville, B.C., Copyright Tim Lilburn 1986. "The Green Lobe of God's Brain, Country From St. John's Sideroad North to Lake Simcoe" and "Chant for the Feast of St. Francis" from *Tourist to Ecstasy* by Tim Lilburn reprinted by permission of Tim Lilburn and Exile Editions, Toronto, Copyright Tim Lilburn 1989 and Exile Editions. "In the Hills, Watching," "Contemplation is Mourning," "Discipline of Secrecy," "Going into the Cloud," "Gazing at the Wall" and "Restoration" from *Moosewood Sandhills* by Tim Lilburn reprinted by permission of Tim Lilburn and McClelland & Stewart, Inc. The Canadian Publishers, Toronto, Copyright Tim Lilburn 1994. The interview was conducted through written correspondence with the editor from Nov. of 1996 to Jan. 1997, printed by permission of author, Copyright Tim Lilburn 1996.

DANIEL DAVID MOSES: "To Susan," "Evensong After Rain," "Post Memoriam" and "A Spider Song" from *Delicate Bodies* by Daniel David Moses reprinted by permission of Daniel David Moses and Nightwood Editions, Sechelt, B.C., Copyright Daniel David Moses 1992; originally published by blewointment press (1980). "The Corn," "The Persistence of Songs," "A Shaman Song Predicting Winter," "Grandmother of the Glacier" and "A Story from the Mouths On a Beach" from *The White Line* by Daniel David Moses reprinted by permission of Daniel David Moses and Fifth House Publishers, Saskatoon, Copyright Daniel David Moses 1990. "A Bone in the Balance of Moonlight," unpublished poem, printed by permission of Daniel David Moses, Copyright Daniel David Moses 1996. The interview was conducted through written correspondence with the author in Dec. 1996, reprinted by permission of author, Copyright Daniel David Moses 1996.

P.K. PAGE: "Stories of Snow," "The Filled Pen," "Three Gold Fish," "For Mstislav Rostropovich with Love," "Chinese Boxes," "About Death," "At Sea" and the essay "Questions and Images," (first published in *Canadian Literature*) from *The Glass Air: Poems Selected and New*, Oxford University Press, Copyright 1991, P.K. Page, reprinted by permission of the author. "Hologram," "Presences," and "Planet Earth" from *Hologram: a Book of Glosas*, Brick Books, Copyright 1994, P.K. Page, reprinted by permission of author.

AJMER RODE: "In Blue Meditation," "Ancestral Museum," "That Name,"

"Still Light," "Heart of the Seed,," "Stroll in a Particle," "Knock Gently," "Yellow Smile," and "The Maharishi and the Baby" from *Blue Meditations* by Ajmer Rode reprinted by permission of Ajmer Rode and Third Eye Publications Inc., (London, Ontario), Copyright Ajmer Rode 1985. "Guru and the Lotus Eyes" and "Playing with Big Numbers" from *Poems at My Doorstep* by Ajmer Rode reprinted by permission of Ajmer Rode and The Caitlin Press (Vancouver, B.C.), Copyright Ajmer Rode 1990. Prose piece by Ajmer Rode published by permission of author, Copyright Ajmer Rode 1997.

ROBIN SKELTON: "Everything," "The Rule," "Knowledge," "Sanctuary," and "Lost," "Names" and "The Witches" from *One Leaf Shaking: Collected Later Poems 1977-1990* by Robin Skelton reprinted by permission of Robin Skelton and Beach Holme Publishers, Victoria, B.C., Copyright Robin Skelton 1996. "To My Sons and Daughters" and "Tao" from *Popping Fuchsias: Poems 1987-1992* by Robin Skelton reprinted by permission of Robin Skelton and CaCanadadada Press (now Ronsdale Press), Copyright 1992 by Robin Skelton. "The Process" and "Finally" from *The Edge of Time: Poems and Translations* by Robin Skelton reprinted by permission of Robin Skelton and Ronsdale\Cacanadadada Press, Copyright Robin Skelton 1995. Interview with Robin Skelton conducted in Jan. 1997 in Victoria, B.C., printed by permission of author, Copyright Robin Skelton 1997.

ANNE SZUMIGALSKI: "Woman Reading in Bath" from *Woman Reading in Bath* by Anne Szumigalski reprinted by permission of Anne Szumigalski, first printed by Doubleday Canada Ltd, Toronto, Copyright Anne Szumigalski 1974. "Angels" from *A Game of Angels* by Anne Szumigalski reprinted by permission of Anne Szumigalski, first printed by Turnstone Press, Winnipeg, Copyright Anne Szumigalski 1980. "Jerusalem," "A Closed Room," and "Annwfn" from *Doctrine of Signatures* by Anne Szumigalski reprinted by permission of Anne Szumigalski, first printed by Fifth House Publishers, Saskatoon, Copyright Anne Szumigalski 1983. "The Compassion" from *Dogstones: Selected and New Poems* by Anne Szumigalski reprinted by permission of Anne Szumigalski, first printed by Fifth House Publishers, Saskatoon, Copyright Anne Szumiglaski 1986. "$i^2=-1$" from *Rapture of the Deep* by Anne Szumigalski reprinted by permission of Anne Szumigalski and Coteau Books, Copyright Anne Szumigalski 1991. "Malus" and "Paradislaan" from *Voice* by Anne Szumigalski with paintings by Marie Elyse St. George, reprinted by permission of Anne Szumigalski and Coteau Books, Copyright Anne Szumigalski 1995. "Between One Thing and Another" by Anne Szumigalski, printed by permission of author, Copyright Anne Szumigalski 1995.

SHARON THESEN: "Easter Sunday" from *Artemis Hates Romance* by Sharon Thesen reprinted by permission of Sharon Thesen; originally published by Coach

House Press, Toronto, Copyright Sharon Thesen 1980. "The Plenitudes" from *Holding the Pose* by Sharon Thesen reprinted by permission of Sharon Thesen, originally published by Coach House Press, Toronto, Copyright Sharon Thesen 1983. "The Stone," "The Shroud of Turin," "Rosary," "Poem for Norbert's Thesis," and "Mythology" from *The Pangs of Sunday* by Sharon Thesen reprinted by permission of Sharon Thesen and McClelland & Stewart Inc., Toronto, The Canadian Publishers, Copyright Sharon Thesen 1990. "The Stone," "The Shroud of Turin" and "Rosary" appeared previously in *The Beginning of the Long Dash* (1987). "The Broken Cup," "After Roy Kiyooka's Funeral," and "Aurora" from *Aurora* by Sharon Thesen reprinted by permission of Sharon Thesen, originally published by Coach House Press, Toronto, Copyright Sharon Thesen 1995. "A Bibliography of Spirit" by Sharon Thesen published by permission of author, Copyright 1997.

MIRIAM WADDINGTON: All poems in this anthology are from *Miriam Waddington: Collected Poems* by Miriam Waddington reprinted by permission of Miriam Waddington and Oxford University Press, Toronto, Copyright Miriam Waddington 1986. Interview conducted in Vancouver, B.C. Dec. 1996, printed by permission of Miriam Waddington, Copyright Miriam Waddington 1996.

DAVID ZIEROTH: "This Side" from *When the Stones Fly Up* by Dale [David] Zieroth reprinted by permission of David Zieroth and House of Anansi, Toronto, Copyright Dale Zieroth 1985. "Function of the Individual," "Thinking My Neighbour's Thoughts," "Once Again Among the Humans," "On the Path of Inner Development," and "The Mouse and My Mother" from *How I Joined Humanity At Last*, reprinted by permission of David Zieroth and Harbour Publshing, Copyright 1998. "Function of the Individual" was published in *Canadian Literature*; "Thinking My Neighbour's Thoughts" in *Poetry Canada*, and "On the Path of Inner Development" in *Pottersfield Portfolio*. "The Poplars of St. Vital," "Separation," "Question" and "Three Trees" are from an unpublished manuscript by David Zieroth printed by permission of author, Copyright 1998. "The Poplars of St. Vital" was published in *Grain*; "Three Trees" in *Event*. "The Gulf of Heaven" is an unpublished poem reprinted by permission of the author, Copyright 1998. Prose piece "Spirit and Poetry" by David Zieroth printed by permission of author, Copyright David Zieroth 1998.

About The Editor

Susan McCaslin is a poet and instructor of English and Creative Writing at Douglas College in New Westminster, B.C. She completed her M.A. at Simon Fraser University (1973) and her doctorate at UBC (1984), both in English literature, and has been a long-time student of comparative religions, mythology, mysticism and mystical theology. She is the author of four books of poetry: *Locutions* (Ekstasis, 1995), *Light Housekeeping* (Ekstasis, 1997), *Veil\Unveil* (St. Thomas Poetry Series, 1997), and *Letters to William Blake* (M[O]ther Tongue Press, 1997). She is the first-place winner of the 1997 M[O]ther Tongue Chapbook Contest for *Letters to William Blake.* She resides in Port Moody, British Columbia with her husband and daughter.

Printed in November 1998 by
VEILLEUX
ON DEMAND PRINTING INC.
in Boucherville, Quebec